P9-BZZ-578

COME
TO
THE
PARTY

Other Books by KARL A. OLSSON

Things Common and Preferred
Seven Sins and Seven Virtues
Passion
By One Spirit
The God Game

Karl A. Olsson

COME TO THE PARTY

An Invitation to a Freer Life Style

WORD BOOKS, Publisher
Waco, Texas

COME
TO
THE
PARTY

Library of Congress catalog card no.: 72–84167

Printed in the United States of America

Continued on page 6.

To
Sally
and all the other blessed
who, long before me,
understood that there was
a party

Acknowledgments

This book would have been impossible without the friends I have encountered through Laity Lodge and Faith at Work. I have spoken of my indebtedness to Myron C. Madden. I am also grateful to Bruce Larson, Ralph Osborne, Heidi Frost, Walden Howard, and Stanley Jones for reading the manuscript and making helpful suggestions. My immediate family has also contributed their insights to this my most personal book.

Paula Breen has typed the manuscript and helped me through many revisions. I am greatly in her debt.

I would also like to thank the following:

The Macmillan Company for permission to quote from Edwin Arlington Robinson, "Nicodemus," from *Collected Poems of Edwin Arlington Robinson,* copyright 1932 by Edwin Arlington Robinson, renewed 1960 by Ruth Nivison and Barbara R. Holt.

Mrs. Arthur Guiterman for permission to quote from Arthur Guiterman's "Hills."

Mrs. Norma Millay Ellis for permission to quote from Edna St. Vincent Millay's "God's World," copyright 1917, 1945 by Edna St. Vincent Millay, Harper & Row, *Collected Poems.*

Contents

Introduction

The most difficult thing about writing this book has been finding a title which said what I meant to say. I suppose I could have called it a "theology of grace" or "the quest for blessing," but both of those titles would have been cop-outs. I needed to invite people to the party.

Why did I find it so difficult? For two reasons, I think. In the first place I am a Christian living in a world full of sin, shame, suffering, hospitals, concentration camps, prisons, mental institutions, war and violence, greed and corruption, flippancy and heartlessness. I belong to a people with fat hearts and fat bodies, docile, insensitive, pouty, and delicate—what Amos called the "kine of Bashan."

How can I even think about a party in a world either choked to death with parties or starved to death with poorness: the despair both of unwant and of want?

When I was a child we used to call church parties socials because, I suppose, the word "party" sounded worldly. At a social you could be decorously jolly but certainly not hilarious. Today we have a different kind of sobriety. The judgment I used to see in the faces of some of my pious elders I now see in the faces of the concerned young.

How, in the midst of all the miseries and the miserables, can we talk about a party?

The justification lies in the language and acts of Jesus. He was, despite the sad world he inhabited and the solemn destiny which lay coiled in him, the prime host and the prime guest of the party. He ate and drank; he let himself be doused with perfume; he was concerned about wedding wine and wedding garments. Without denying anything that was sad or sinful, bloody or pallid, Jesus was indeed Lord of the Feast.

My second reason for hesitating about the title is more personal. I am, in some sense which will become apparent in this book, not a blessed child. I am not Joseph of the coat of many colors. Hence I could never feel that I belonged at a party. It was my lot to serve and to suffer, not to enjoy myself. That does not mean that I did not go to parties (most of them innocent) and enjoy myself while there. There were moments when in the perfumed presence of the young girls—so pink and white of flesh and so ravishingly fair of form—I was close to ecstasy. But something somber in me held back. I nearly always felt that the party was not for me, that when the clock struck I would end up in the chimney corner.

Despite these reservations, I have managed to risk a title which in some ways frightens and embarrasses me. And I can risk it because through Jesus (O beautiful and banal phrase) I have discovered that I too am a child of blessing and belong at the party. And that I need never go away.

I have also discovered that the church is the new family of blessing, that is, the New Israel, and that the presupposition of its life is the grace of the party. I do not believe that the church exists for mission as if it were an army of workers, gray, stolid, and joyless. I believe that the church exists for joy in relationship. It is made by love for love. Furthermore, I believe that grace begets both gracefulness and graciousness.

Accountability for the world is born in love, not guilt. When we are truly at the party, we want to see the house full.

Hence, when I invite you to the party, though I do so shyly and with the diffidence of a newcomer, I feel no guilt. I am not inviting you to a freaked-out corner of the cosmos but to a new heaven and a new earth, which are really the old heaven and the old earth all dressed up for the party.

Part I

THE BLISS OF THE PARTY

| Chapter 1 | The Blessed |

The Girl in the Blue Velvet Dress

One of my earliest experiences of bliss was a party.

I was very young—no more than six—and retain only a scattering of images: a cold winter night with an infinity of stars; the sense of crowded warmth when we came into the house of my grocer uncle, whose shop so closely adjoined the rooms that the latter were filled with the scent of cheese, coffee, kerosene, freshly milled flour, and raisins; the good smooth feel of my brown velvet suit which contrasted with the eternal pickiness of my everyday pants; the bloom of candlelight and the yellow glow of oil lamps (it was before the days of electricity in the village); and the overall air of festivity. There were food and drink and candy and nuts—mysterious treasures in silver paper—and there was an ancient pianoforte in peeling birch veneer with a pair of tipsy candles, on which someone was banging out Christmas songs. There were also boisterous games, some of which were too complicated for me to follow. I loved the laughing—the red faces, the roars and shrieks. But my most vivid impression was of a young girl—fourteen or fifteen—with hair the color of wheat and a dress of blue velvet. In some game which was passing me by she rescued me. She picked me up and put me in her lap.

I am sure there was something in her act which spoke to my childhood sexuality. It was important to me that she was a girl in blue velvet, blonde and tender, but there were other feelings. She made me feel that I belonged to her. Because of her, I felt that I belonged at the party. Something truly beautiful, warm, and human flowered in me. I was happy to be myself, happy to be a boy, and happy to be where I was. The black earth and the sky of stars enveloping the little illuminated box where we feasted were themselves in celebration. I sensed even then that a bigger party was going on. As we walked home toward our house at the edge of the village, I remember asking my father what the stars were. He answered me with a whimsy. They were lamps in the palaces of heaven. That night the lamps were lit over the earth for me, and I walked in sleepy wonder at the glory of things, remembering forever the bliss of the party and the grace of the young girl who had given me a gift.

Red Balloons

The Bible is a party full of merriment and red balloons. The feast outruns the fast. Andrew Lang once called *The Odyssey* "the eatingest book," but the Bible doesn't take a second place. It is crammed with spitted kids and lambs and fatted calves; oil in the beard, bread and cakes; grapes, pomegranates, olives, dates; skins and vats of wine; milk and honey. It abounds in party clothes, perfumes, and ointments; in music, dancing, and frolic. Jesus came and wherever he went there was a party, "the feast of the bridegroom" (Luke 7:31-34, RSV). Or there was a party and Jesus was there. It would be tedious to list all the allusions to feasting, but the parables of Jesus are full of it, and it is significant that the last gathering of the disciples was a celebration. The Bible's first words have to do with the splendor of a garden filled with fruit trees, and its closing words are an invitation to the party.

> Happy are those who wash their robes clean, and so have the right to eat the fruit from the tree of life, and to go through the gates into the city. . . . I, Jesus, have sent my angel to announce these things to you in the churches. I am the descendant from the family of David; I am the bright morning star. The Spirit and the Bride say, "Come!" Everyone who hears this must also say, "Come!" Come, whoever is thirsty; accept the water of life as a gift, whoever wants it (Rev. 22:14-17, TEV).

But the Bible is also filled with jealous eyes and malicious hearts. It is crammed with stories of intrigue, envy, and even murder. There are fasters who think ill of feasters. There are workers who think ill of partyers. There are brothers who never made it hating the brother who did. There is sweetness in the Bible, song and celebration. But there are also bitterness and rage, the sound of weeping and the gnashing of teeth. There is blessing, but it does not neutralize the cursing. "Jacob have I loved, but Esau have I hated" (Rom. 9:13).

What is the meaning of it all? What does it mean to feel that existence with all its agony, its hollow places, its sickening doubt, its nothingness, its despair, its sins and warpings is still, despite this, a party? Conversely what does it mean to feel that no matter how well I order my life, do my work and pay my debts, no matter how elegantly I furnish existence and contrive celebration, I never make it? What is it to be blessed, to be unblessed?

Calves and Kids

There is a well-known story in the New Testament which has a first meaning and a second meaning. It is the story of the lost son (which traditionally has been translated "prodigal" in the English versions) and the elder brother. The first meaning of the story is obviously that God loves us no matter how far we stray from him, and that when we have messed things up, he not only waits for us but comes running toward us and welcomes us back with a joyous celebration. When we accept that meaning, we see that the father's character is much more clearly perceived by the lost and restored son than by the brother who stayed home and needed no restoration.

But there is a second meaning in the story. For the son who goes away is clearly the blessed son. That is, he is the child who is so secure in his father's love and favor that he is free to claim his share of the property, free to go away and squander it, free to mess his life up generally, but also free enough to repent and return and join in the celebration meant for him.

The son who stays home, on the other hand, is the unblessed. He is not free to do anything. All his life he has fearfully searched the face of his father for signs of approval and disapproval. Unconsciously he knows that no matter how early he gets up in the morning and how long he works into the night, no matter how moralistically he follows every whim of his father and how scrupulously he takes every suggestion, he will never make it. Insecure, self-hating, compulsive, unblessed, he tries to earn his gifts. He has no freedom to ask anything of his father, not even a kid to make a party with his friends. (We take the liberty to ask, "What party? What friends?") He cannot oppose his father, argue with him (father is always right), charge him with manipulation, even hate him consciously. The elder brother can't go away, can't risk because he can't handle failure (he sweats at the thought), can't externally mess things up. Nor can he repent, return, admit failure, establish new and free relationships, be loved and love, feast until his face is greasy with celebration, be comfortable in outrageously party-ish clothes, dance wildly like a leaf or a wave, or cast himself into the arms of music—soft, martial, sentimental, ingenuous, brassy, jazzy, rocky, mystical, moody—whatever.

The human family—at least what I know of it—is divided into these two groups: the blessed and the unblessed, the favored and the unfavored, the free and the good, those who have come to the party and those who haven't, those who think they can come, and those who think they can't.*

Jacob and Esau

"Bless me, even me also, O my father," is the cry of Esau after Jacob has cheated him of his father's blessing. But Isaac has only one blessing to give.

The story, which occurs in Genesis 27, is an illustration of the mystery of blessing. Isaac and his wife Rebekah are Semitic

---

* In sharing the gospel of the party with people around the country, I have discovered that they fall into four categories:

1. Those who doubt that there is a party.

2. Those who believe that there is a party somewhere, but they're not invited.

3. Those who believe there is a party and they're invited but they don't deserve to stay.

4. Those who are invited and go and stay.

nomads, living in ancient Canaan. They are happy in the birth of twins, of which the first-born is Esau, the second, Jacob. Two special favors belong to the first-born—the birthright and the blessing. The birthright is a promissory note on the lion's share of the family property; the blessing an entering into the sexual potency of the family (the hand under the thigh), an assurance of a productive future, a grasp on the imponderables of tomorrow, an "in" with the right forces, a special kind of luck, a "thing" in relation to God.

Esau has the birthright and will get the blessing when the sexual energies of Isaac are finally depleted. But Jacob, possessing a special élan or spirit, perhaps with the favor of the Most High and certainly with the connivance of his mother Rebekah, cheats Esau of his birthright. He does this by seducing Esau into selling it. Esau is a hunter and one day, like many hunters, misses his chance to eat. Famished, he returns to Jacob's tent. Perhaps he is a gourmet and fond of a special stew which the shrewd Jacob has learned to prepare for him. In any event Esau is stumbling into camp when his nostrils are assailed by the most ravishing smell of sizzling meat and rich marrow gravy. And Jacob, the bargainer, knowing his brother's plight, agrees to sell Esau some pottage for the birthright.

A little later Jacob is ready for the next turn of the screw. He has taken Esau's birthright. Now he is ready to gamble for the blessing. Taking advantage of Isaac's failing eyesight with his mother's urging and help, he dresses himself in goat skins so as to simulate Esau's hairy body. And he softens up old Isaac by bringing him a savory dish. Isaac is not absolutely taken in. He accepts the hairy body as Esau's, but he is not fooled by Jacob's voice. But it may well be, as Thomas Mann suggests, that Isaac *wants* Jacob to have the blessing, he wants to be fooled. And so he confers the blessing on Jacob—a once-and-for-all transaction, unshakable as the mountains.

When Esau discovers the trick, he is dumbfounded. He comes in to Isaac seeking to redress his grievance. But Isaac has chosen. He has no further blessing to give.

To our time, largely unfamiliar with the Bible, this story with its blessing and cursing may seem both harsh and irrelevant. What have we enlightened modern people to do with such crude, archaic knavery?

But are we so different? If we translate the story into modern terms and speak not of blessing and cursing but rather of the "fair-haired boy" and the "black sheep," where is the irrelevance? Could not Jacob and Esau be the twin sons of a twentieth-century father whose struggle to be "just" is as desperate and as hopeless as that of Isaac?

It is a fact that although favoritism is repugnant to us as Westerners, most of us practice it. At the levels below consciousness we know that favoritism exists and that we are often governed by it. The average Western middle-class family, nurtured in the tradition of absolute equality, will try to make sure that the children share equally in the justice and love of father and mother. In such a family the pie will be cut into equal pieces: immunizations, orthodontia, clarinet lessons, snowsuits, baby books of the stages on life's way—all this will be distributed equitably. In the event of the death of the parents, the estate will be so arranged that all three children share and share alike.

Despite this neat parental way of assuring justice, however, the children in the family probably experience something different. At the gut level they sense favoritism. They know who among the children are Jacob and Esau, favored and unfavored. In moments of insight so do the parents.

What is it to be a favored child? In our society, which tries hard to be egalitarian, it does not usually involve a disproportion of goods or even of conscious love. Good parents—and

how desperately the best parents struggle with this problem—
may, in response to their unconscious guilt, try to balance out
everything. They may even overcompensate and try to give the
ugly duckling more swan's-down than all the others. But in
the long run they fool no one. Even with all the white down
shaken upon the duckling—a smothering snow of beneficence
—he still knows himself to be a duckling and not a swan,
never a swan.

A friend once told me of a family he visited in which the
favors were unequally distributed. There was a happy child,
secure in the love of his father, and there was an unhappy one.
The visitor tried to adjust matters by paying particular attention to the unloved child. The child responded greedily to this
affirmation but also with a kind of despair. He knew it wouldn't
make any difference where it counted—in the regard of his
parents.

The visitor in telling me this story revealed his own situation. He also was an unwanted child reared in a family where
he had to observe his brother adored and spoiled while he
picked up only the crumbs which fell from the master's table.
His emotional wound had made him sensitive to the misfor-
tune of being unblessed.

What is the favor we are talking about? What is it to be
blessed? It is a kind of mystery communicated by nonverbal
signs. It is perhaps a promise of particular nearness and particular support. "I will be on your side. Don't be afraid. You
are not forgotten. I'll be around. If there is to be a choice, you
will be the chosen."

Strangely enough the effect of this promise of presence is
freedom for the favored child. The son who is assured of his
father's favor is free from the anxiety of seeking it. The unblessed, on the contrary, live in the bondage of unfulfillment.

They may wander over the face of the earth, but their wandering does not bring them nearer home. They may stay at home but their nearness to the source of blessing does not free them into gladness.

Everything Is Family

At its deepest levels the biblical world is a family. The relationships between God and man, and man and man; the way a man understands himself; even his conception of the world of creatures which surrounds him—all this is couched in the language of the family. The family metaphor is, of course, not limited to the Semitic world. The Greek gods had a primal father and so did the Nordic. Cronus and Odin are the big daddies; primitive religion abounds in earth mothers with ample laps and generous breasts.

But although it is certainly true that the Greek world was rich in family myths, so that we are constantly banging our heads against Oedipus and Electra, the development of Greek thought tended to push the family image into the background. Greek philosophies, although they made free use of the family stories, did not ultimately see the nature of things in these terms. They did not think of existence as a family. They thought of it in such abstract terms as permanence and change; matter, form, and motion; atoms and the void; being and becoming; appearance and reality.

But whereas sophistication for the Greeks meant the abandonment of the family model, in the biblical world the growth of insight resulted in the development and enrichment of that model. It is no accident that the New Testament world sees the people of God as sons and heirs, and as brothers of the "first of many brothers" (Rom. 8:29, TEV). The Bible's first book is dominated by family relationships. The first beginnings of things are familial, and in every family situation there is election, choice, blessing.

At the rational level there seems no easy way of accounting for this chosenness. Devotees of an evolutionary sociology a half-century ago noted that the pastoral figures seemed to get a better deal. That would account for Abel's being preferred to Cain. Abel was a shepherd; Cain was a farmer. In the case of Jacob and Esau we have the shepherd and the hunter juxtaposed, with the shepherd again coming out in the favored position. But this kind of argument won't do. Especially does it not reckon with the profound and vexing relationship between the father and the first-born.

The status of the first-born son in primitive societies is a complex problem, for from one point of view he is the favored one. Not only is he first on the scene; his firstness allows him to establish himself as the heir apparent before his rivals appear to challenge him. And even when his brothers and sisters populate the kingdom where he formerly enjoyed his solitary status, is he not by virtue of his age and experience and presumed wisdom the natural prince—the first—in the family? So generally accepted is the standing of the first-born son that in many societies the right of primogeniture existed until the most recent times. The oldest son inherited the farm, the estate, or the family's trade or profession as a matter of course. In all remaining Western monarchies this right is still scrupulously observed.

But the first-born is at the same time a source of intense pain to the father. For while, on the one hand, he is the best guarantee for the continuation of the family—he is, so to speak, the bridge to the future—he is on the other hand a reminder to the father of the latter's mortality. The oldest son waits in the anteroom of power for nature to take its course. At least this is what the father unconsciously feels.

Hence the rather common embarrassment and awkwardness in the relationship of fathers to their first-born sons. The son is the son of promise no doubt. "Let your servant go in peace" (Luke 2:29, TEV). The son means the continuity of the family and the race. But he is also a threat, for his ascent means the descent of the father. "The king is dead; long live the king."

Out of such feelings for the first-born, complicated unquestionably by the Oedipal situation explored by Freud and his successors, may come the tendency within biblical society to confer the blessing on one of the other children.*

But whatever the nature of the machinery which brings about this distribution of favor, the fact remains that in the biblical world the truth of the dictum "Jacob have I loved, but Esau have I hated" is everywhere seen.

Blessing and Testing

The favored son in the Old Testament world is a manifestation of the joy and freedom of grace. The chosen one

* It is a curious fact that in the Bible the blessing or the favor seldom goes to the first-born. Primitive Semitic society seems to have made a conscious effort to redress the imbalance by conferring rights on the first-born. But such natural rights are seldom equated with the blessing. Cain is the first-born, so are Ishmael, Esau, and Reuben. But the beloved are Abel, Isaac, Jacob, and Joseph. When Jacob is about to die and is blessing the sons of Joseph, he deliberately crosses his hands so as to put his right hand on the head of Ephraim, the younger son. This is contrary to the conscious wishes of Joseph. He tries to give the blessing to the older son. But Jacob, the grandfather, prevails.

It is tempting to see in this curious incident Jacob's recapitulation of his own blessing at the hands of Isaac when he had, in effect, been responsible for crossing Isaac's hands. Does Joseph in this instance respond to his own guilt as the blessed younger son?

knows that he enjoys his status because of the mystery of election; it is a gift which he cannot merit and yet the gift makes him more lovable and so still more blessed.

Despite the decorum observed by Abraham and the beautiful spiritual discipline which he everywhere observes, it is clear that he acts out of the security and freedom which come from knowing that he is loved. His exodus from Haran is often pointed to as an act of faith. This it certainly is. More than that, however, it is the act of a man who is confident that God has proclaimed his love for him, that there has been a contract established between God and him which reads, "Because I have loved you, you will love to serve me."

Abraham's security, which is manifested so clearly in his dealings with Lot, is rooted in this sense of blessedness. He seems to know that in his dealings with his warring neighbors, his family, and even his future he has an unassailable position; he dwells in a mighty fortress. A further evidence of this security is his refusal to question his position. Abraham worries about Sodom and Gomorrah but not about himself. Even in the probation (the sacrifice of Isaac, to which we shall return later), there is no neurasthenic grubbing into the question of God's intent with this embarrassing demand. Unlike Jeremiah who keeps digging into God's curious ways with him, Abraham maintains a kind of grave composure very close to merriment. I am not at all sure, for example, that the laughter of Sarah and Abraham arises from true unbelief. I see it rather as the surprised snort of people who are always being surprised by a God who cannot be charted or confined to a formula, but who is always the great novelty.

The freedom of the blessing is a risky business, and it should not surprise us that the blessed people are subject to special temptations such as vanity, pride, willfulness, disorderliness, thoughtlessness, and prodigality. There is little of this in Abraham, but Jacob is heedless and even cruel, and Joseph's attitude toward his brothers is marked by narcissistic self-love, vanity, and a naïveté about trampling on the feelings of others which would be amazing if we did not see it in the context of the blessing.

Israel, as the chosen people, historically manifests the same characteristics as the favored child. The election, which is a gift to be held in gratitude and humility, in the history of Israel becomes a right and thus the basis of the most intolerable self-vaunting. The prophets never weary of telling Israel that the covenant with God is conditional and that the blessing can and will be removed if they persist in their arrogance.

It is in this context of the risk of blessing that the "test" must be seen. The writer to the Hebrews tells first-century Christians that "whom the Lord loves he chastens." In biblical history God tests the blessed child, not the unblessed. It is Abraham who must take his blessed child to the mountain to be sacrificed. It is Jacob who must labor for fourteen years for the girl he loves. It is Joseph who is sold into Egypt, harassed by the wife of Potiphar, and thrown into a dungeon. Job, who represents a most obvious example of the man of blessing, is subjected to misfortunes of an overwhelming sort.

Now this suffering is not punishment for a specific sin. It is not even atonement. It is chastening, probation, testing. It is intended to alert the blessed one to the fact that love is sometimes, in Dante's words, a "lord of terrible aspect," the harshness and pain of which are intended to render the beloved more lovable. Job says quite rightly, "He [God] knows the way that I take; when he has tried me, I shall come forth as gold" (Job 23:10, RSV).

Chapter 2

The Seekers of Blessing

The Voice of Woe

It must be obvious that not all the characters in the Old Testament have the same relaxed attitude toward God and their own situation. In fact biblical history manifests a second mentality of an entirely different order. There are the patriarchs and there are the prophets, and the difference between the two is that the patriarchs have the blessing while most of the prophets seek it.

In the category of the prophets I would like to include the lawmakers as well as the more traditional proclaimers. (Moses is a special case—a beautiful anomaly—because he is so reluctant about his job, so inconsistent and wonderfully volcanic in his leadership, and so marvelously free in grousing to God. Because Moses seems secure, I shall ask that he be placed among the blessed.) Many of the other prophets have a real hang-up on God. They see it as their task to speak the word of malediction—the "Woe, woe" for God—and I have no doubt that God uses them to chasten his people and to train his children. Law and thunder and woes and "we view with alarm" are pedagogically useful, or God would not permit them to exist, but the people who are vehicles of this judgment seem to fall into the category of the unblessed. They come through to me as terribly unhappy people who have fallen off the bus and are trying to explain how to get back on. They are the unblessed children who have translated their disappointment into oughtness. Often they are the "no-no" people who prophesy, not out of terrible necessity, but out of a delight in straightening others out.

An image floats to the surface of my memory. Somewhere in the web of our large and unwieldy relations and what seems like a hundred years ago, some children are playing on the floor of a large empty barn. They are silly like most children; they run, they leap, and a few start whirling around in a dance. But they are children of a strict pietistic family and in the midst of their celebration they are interrupted. An older brother stands primly in the door. He has come from nowhere. He lifts a finger and warns like the budding prophet he is, "Just wait, I am telling father about this."

It is possible to recognize in this stiff, unhappy creature millions of religionists who busy themselves with God's expectations in a fussy, meddlesome way because they are unhappy about being rejected and unblessed. "Jacob have I loved, but Esau have I hated." How many Esaus there are who have become meticulous in their religious observance, tedious and paranoid in their evaluations of other people's goodness, sadistic in leveling judgment and assigning punishment because some-where in their existence there was a Jacob who walked off with the birthright and the blessing.

It would be unscientific and unfair to conclude that all or most clergymen are unblessed children who seek to compen-sate for their lack of favor by working terribly hard at being good. But if I draw on my own experience, I have to conclude that many ministers I know and many so-called "dedicated laymen" are unblessed. They may deserve a goat and a party, but they lack the security to ask for it. Hence they wear them-selves out in a tiresome and unrewarding round of activities. They stay near the father and carry out their work under his nose, but they are never very happy, and when anyone is too happy around them, they feel frustrated and envious.

The unblessed minister used to be the preacher of judgment who came down hard on the worldliness of his congregation and excoriated the flock for its vanity, greed, lust, and impiety. Now he is inclined to be the joiner of causes, the social activist, the protester who expresses his unhappiness with himself by raging at the world and taking the church to task.

The Unblessed Child

I know a great deal about the unblessed minister, for I am one myself. I feel that I got my father's love but not his favor. All my life I have stayed at home in the father's house, devot-ing myself to religious interests of one kind or another. I have been a pastor, a chaplain, a teacher and administrator in a Christian college and seminary. The five years I spent in teach-ing and administration on a university campus were confusing for me because I didn't feel that I belonged. I felt disloyal to the church and to the Christian enterprise, which had claimed my loyalty.

When I examine this vocational pattern more closely, I

become convinced that my whole life has been devoted to a search for the blessing which I could never secure. I was one with the elder brother, convinced with him that if I did my homework and the chores, learned to tie the right knots and earn the right merit badges, and if I didn't carouse around and waste my substance but deposited my paychecks, some day I would make it and have the calf, the candles, and the party.

In saying this, I want in no way to reflect on the home from which I come. From every point of view it was an ideal home, and I am sure that those of my friends who know something of the circumstances in which I grew up will consider any reflection on that household to be evidence not only of ingratitude, but of a kind of madness. Imagine, if you will, a home in which the father fulfilled all the requirements of his role. He was energetic, innovative, intelligent, strong, witty, noble, beautifully organized, unselfish, and in his way, loving. Although he was gone for four of my first nine years for extended periods of time, when he was home he was generous with his time and his attention. I still retain copies of letters which he wrote to us children when his work took him away from us—at one time for over twenty months. These letters were calibrated to our understanding; they were informative, and even when they slipped into didacticism and piety, as they frequently did, they breathed affection and gentleness.

From my ninth year until I left for college, we were pretty much together as a family. During this time Sunday was family day, and after worshiping together, we would frequently take long walks, go on picnics, or visit the parks, the museums, and art collections of the city in which we lived. I even recall that the mild Sabbatarianism of our home was occasionally relaxed to allow us to go to an amusement park together.

There are other memories of my father. When we were assailed by nightmares, he frequently comforted us. I remember hearing his reassuring voice beside my bed in the dark of the night. Occasionally when he gave rein to his inherited gift of humor and mimicry and embarked on sharing an incredible repertoire of stories and anecdotes, we were enthralled. When he was gone from home we genuinely missed him and prayed for our reunion.

For us children he was the adequate man. On Sunday mornings when he awakened us for Sunday school and church, he would invent kindly ways of springing us loose from sleep. He would give us a tune on his violin, which he played tolerably well, or he would sing a few bars of a song which celebrated the joys of morning. He seems to have acted on the assumption that bad morning temper was a mild demon possession which would respond to the exorcism of music and good humor.

Dad was the one who trimmed our finger- and toe-nails and who managed the bad knots in our shoelaces. I recall a sleepy lurching walk through the woods when I was not more than five. We had visited a neighboring farm and had to walk home in the dark November night. We were not carried, for there was a tradition in the family that only infants were carried. I remember collapsing on my bed when we eventually made it home. I wanted to get undressed but I was hobbled by badly knotted shoelaces. The sense of security and release which my father's strong, sure fingers, at work on the laces, gave me was really beautiful.

Despite this fair cluster of memories from the life of a good, wise man, I felt rather early that I was not in his favor. I wanted to be, but I was not. Although he loved me, I did not manage to please him. At least I felt this.

My father and mother both came out of the Swedish free church tradition. They had been reared and confirmed in the

National Church of Sweden which was doctrinally Lutheran and which in those days baptized and gathered in all the people of Sweden unless they were foreigners or avowed sectaries. But rather early they had come to conversion and new life in Christ and had become affiliated with the Mission Covenant Church of Sweden. The latter church—or association—was doctrinally rather free, but its life style was strongly pietistic. It emphasized the importance of the new birth and of a daily life committed totally to the will of God.

I mention this because the *modus operandi* in our household was to refer all major decisions and many minor ones to the operation of the divine will. My parents were steeped in the Bible, and some of the tedium of our childhood years came from hours of Bible study, which my father seems to have enjoyed hugely but which placed an unbelievable strain on our tender minds and particularly on our bottoms. The emphasis in the study, however, was never doctrinal. There was a heady theological freedom around my parents which was a pleasant contrast to the orthodoxy of some of the people in our communion who were committed to a hardening fundamentalism. Hence, when we developed an interest we were allowed to discuss theology with great heat and with a wide margin of tolerance. But in one area the conviction remained firm: to be a Christian meant to search out and commit oneself to the will of God.

My father was interested in the whole Bible, but the figure of the obedient Christ who lovingly took up his cross to suffer and die for us was always at center stage. To do the will of God was to carry one's cross. If I had not been so eager to make it with my father, I would probably have taken the injunction to cross-bearing less seriously. But because this was so central for him, I made it central in my own life. As I look back on

33

the decisions of my late adolescence, I see them as affected at each point by the need to serve and to suffer.

By this I do not mean that I was subservient to all of my father's wishes. I was ego-strong and in some areas I broke away from the pietistic patterns in which my parents lived. I was interested in literature and refused to apply the standard of usefulness to what I read. As a junior and again as a senior in high school I broke the family tradition by attending school dances. And I argued heatedly for a liberalization of the life style in which I felt we were trapped.

But in the primal outlines of my life, my basic geology, I was still seeking for God's purposes for me. And I continued to associate this purpose not with freedom and creativity but with cross-bearing, limitation, suffering, and even death. During my last year in high school when I was tempted to become a lawyer and a politician or a journalist and poet, I was constantly drawn back to a more humble and obscure existence by the image of the suffering Christ. I was trying to live out the lines of a gospel song frequently sung in our circle:[1]

> Close to Thee, close to Thee,
> Gladly would I toil and suffer,
> Only let me walk with Thee.*

* When I was a sophomore in college, Robinson's *Nicodemus* was published. Nicodemus's word to Caiaphas about Jesus spoke profoundly to me:

> "High men like you and me,
> Whether by worth or birth or
> Other worldly circumstance,
> Have risen to shining heights,
> And there may still rise higher,
> Where they shall be no higher than earth.
> Men who are braver may forego their shining,
> Leaving it all above them, and go down
> To lowliness and peace, and there find life."
> —Edwin Arlington Robinson
> *Nicodemus, A Book of Poems*
> (New York: The Macmillan Co., 1932), p. 3

We were associated, after coming to America in 1922, with the Evangelical Covenant Church, which was cognate with the Mission Covenant of Sweden. I feel comfortable with the theological posture of the Covenant denomination and have remained associated with it all my life. But in my younger years the Covenant Church was ethnically oriented and, hence, limited both in numbers and in geographical distribution. Despite this parochialism, once I decided to commit myself to the will of God, I saw my life mission as carried out only within my own fellowship. On occasion, in order to explain my position, I would quote the words of the 137th Psalm, "If I forget thee, O Jerusalem, let my right hand forget her cunning" (Ps. 137:5).

I now understand that what kept me devoted to my denomination during so many years of my life was a curious searching not only for the will of God, although that was sincere enough, but for the blessing of my father. I had taken his exhortations on cross-bearing with utmost seriousness and had interpreted such cross-bearing as a ministry limited to my own denomination. By a curious irony, my father did not want me to be a minister nor did he want me to limit my sphere of activity to the denomination and its institutions.

What he wanted me to be and do in particular I never learned. What I probably responded to in him was something he could not articulate in terms of a vocational path. In what I chose to do I was responding to signals in him which often lay beneath the level of his consciousness. What these signals seemed to suggest to me for much of my career was the virtue of unhappiness or the satisfaction of suffering. As I review the decisions of my life, it seems to me that most of them were made against the grain of my nature. I did things not because I wanted to do them or felt particularly qualified to do them but because they were tough and thorny and needed to be done. And in doing or trying to do the tough and thorny, I was hoping I could make it with my father.

Dad is still living and if he were able to read what I have written, I am sure that he would see things very differently. He might protest that he never intended to have such an effect on me and that I have imagined things in him which never existed. This may all be true. I am not building any sort of case against my father. God forbid! I am simply stating what I felt about him and how desperately I sought the blessing he could not give me. That he was not conscious of this and did not consent to it does not alter my feelings.

At one level of understanding he would know very well what it is I am talking about. For he was one of the first to talk to me about the favored child. He asked me once if I had noticed how unfair families are in selecting this or that child for special attention. And he talked often to me about the story of Joseph and his brothers. It was a story which moved him deeply. When the great *Joseph* series by Thomas Mann was first translated, I suggested that he read it, and he finished all the volumes except the last. I believe it was the only major work of fiction my father ever read, though he loved books and was an avid reader.

I used to wonder what it was in the Joseph story which spoke so deeply to my father. He was certainly not the blessed child. He never made it with his father. He used to tell me about his ugly-duckling childhood spent among children who all seemed more charming than he. The Joseph story probably appealed to him because he wanted so much to be Joseph, sporting a coat of many colors and making it big. He also wanted to be in a position where he could forgive his brothers and thus be free of them. But he never made it. Although brighter, better educated, and on the whole more successful than any of them, he lived uneasily among his siblings and seemed relieved that most of his life was spent an ocean away from them.

The Burden of the Elder Brother

I was thus the unblessed child of an unblessed child, and I entered into adult life with the burden of the elder brother on my back. I never asked seriously what my talents were and where in the world I could develop them. My years of university study were carried out without the hope of ever making it in the academic world. I knew instinctively that whatever my academic laurels, I would ultimately have to lay them at the foot of the cross. Hence much of my university life was a sort of game. I did my work seriously enough and completed a doctorate at a prestige university where I taught and administered while I was writing my dissertation. But when my colleagues talked about lines of inquiry and fields of study and promising careers on university campuses, I felt out of it. I was like a man dying of an incurable disease. The world of sun and flowers was not for me, at least not for long. I was really saying to myself, "If I had the choice of this or that academic career, these would be my opportunities. But of course I have no choice."

While I was still doing undergraduate work at the university, I was whirled away into a temporary pastorate. Though I was only twenty at the time and would have had every excuse to cut my time short, I stayed on in the pastorate for over a year. After a year of university studies, I went to another church and tried for several years to satisfy my ambitions for an advanced degree while I was involved in caring for a medium-sized city parish. After completing my master's degree, I went on to teach in my denominational college and seminary (I could not forget Jerusalem), and after four years volunteered for service as an army chaplain. Back from the service, I completed the doctorate but was no sooner finished with that, than I returned to my denominational seminary where I remained for over twenty years, first as a teacher and then as president.

I have recounted these facts not to nourish my self-pity (for I am not pitiable) but to help me understand what it was that kept me splintered all those years. Part of me wanted and needed a distinguished career in scholarship as a way of actualizing my gifts and fulfilling my destiny. But part of me fought down such ambitions and sought instead the meekness, the obscurity, and perhaps the safety of a religious vocation. It is now clear to me that without knowing it, I was recapitulating the life of the elder brother, and in Myron Madden's packed phrase, repeating the atonement instead of accepting it.

Before documenting my thesis further I would like to make clear that I do not think all service and suffering unnecessary or the mere outworking of sick compulsions. The difference between unblessed and blessed work is freedom and the security that freedom brings. Christ endured the cross because of the joy that was set before him. Paul both served and suffered gladly, and St. Francis, whom I am just now beginning to understand, became a little brother through an excess of love. All acted in freedom, and that makes the difference.

The naked St. Francis in freedom followed the naked Christ. But I did not. My divesting myself of the garments of the flesh was proud, gloomy, and compulsive. As I indicated earlier, I became the pastor of a medium-sized city parish in my early twenties. Almost at the same time I married. Sally and I had attended junior college and university together and had discussed many and varied topics, but, as far as I can remember, we had never talked about who we were or the effect we had on one another. She was an open and sunny nature who was attracted, she now tells me, by a certain ego strength in me. I seemed to be the sort of person who knew what he wanted, and this decisiveness appealed to her. I loved her because she was beautiful, intelligent, and gracious, but also because she was the catch of the campus—a kind of trophy—and I always had to win first prize. I do not think I seriously shared with her what my feeling about the ministry was, and I dragged her with me into projects which she understood well enough but to which she had never become emotionally committed.

Our very first Christmas in the parsonage I invited home for dinner and all the jolly holly a forgotten parishioner whom I discovered living in a miserable wooden shack in the slummiest part of the city. Her little house was lit by kerosene and papered with newspapers reporting the election of FDR and the kidnapping of the Lindbergh baby. She had no running water and obviously no inside toilet. When I found her on a gloomy November afternoon, she peered out at me from exophthalmic eyes and was overwhelmed by confusion and fear. Her shack and she were both filthy and crawling with bedbugs, but I was so needy a person that I could not resist the temptation to set things right at once. Without thinking of how she would feel about it, or how Sally would react, I invited the lady home for Christmas dinner. I am now convinced that I did what I did because I needed the hair-shirt discomfort, the sandpapering and flagellation of this gratuitously good act. It was a work I was carrying out in my effort to secure the blessing. It did not occur to me that I had fallen victim to the worst kind of "Christmas Carol" beneficence, and that I was dealing with my own guilt rather than the poor old lady's discomfort.

Another equally dramatic but even more wooden benevolence was my securing a cataract operation for an old parishioner who combined stinginess and greed with a certain kind
of wheedling manipulativeness. Sally and I and some members
of the church whose aid we solicited took the old man out of
his flophouse, accompanied him through the tedious routine of
registration and examination at the state hospital, waited
through surgery, visited him in his austere hospital room
(even on Christmas Day), and ultimately brought him home
to the parsonage. He was probably the most ornery and un-
grateful person who has ever felt the terrible weight of my
compassion. On my Christmas Day visit, I asked him if I
could buy him something to celebrate the blessed season and he
asked for a fifteen-cent package of Cut Plug. I made the
mistake of buying him a fifty-cent bag, and he was so furious
that I had disobeyed his order that he filled the air with cursing.

When he was ready to leave the hospital and had begun to
see men like trees walking, I brought him home to the
parsonage for what I thought would be a brief transitional
period. He responded by settling in. Time would fail me were
I to relate the full effects of my misguided compassion. I
finally had to tell him to go. Before he submerged himself once
more in the jungle of rejects and winos, he told me what he
thought of my Christian benevolence. Since, at the time of his
operation, I had asked him if he had any safe-deposit box or
bank account which he wanted to tell me about, he assumed
that my motive for helping him was greed, and he added this
suspicion to the list of negations. In his funny warped way he
was right. For though the venal motive he thought he discerned was far from me, my real motives for helping him were
certainly suspect.

I have just been reading an article in a Lutheran publication about the new breed of pastors, an article which informs us that the new pastor "will have no part with [*sic*] deception or hypocrisy, going through the motions and playing games with God." I find myself smiling ironically, for thirty or more years ago that was the way I saw myself. I was going to be God's instrument to cut through the accumulated blubber of a soft, dishonest pietism which cared only for the rich neighbor. I was the scalpel which God had sharpened to do his work in the church. Like St. Francis and Robin Hood, I would be the friend of God's poor. I would leave the softly lit sanctuary with its accumulation of minks and sensuous perfumes and would serve in cheap hotels with a smell of human sweat, bad booze, and Lysol, or in shanties with broken windows and sifting soot, or in hospital wards with flaking paint, or on distant battlefields. Alas, I did not then see that all this nobility was only a response to my inner state. Inside of me there were flophouses and shanties and lazar houses and bloody fields, an aching, dreary, unblessed continent. I was the elder brother squinting over the dusty fields, wielding a tired sickle, hating the sun and the earth and myself.

In the midst of all this my health gave way. I couldn't go another step, and appropriately I developed a crippling ailment in my knee, a mysterious something which allowed me to hobble out of an impossible vocation with grace. Although I had read some Freud, and Weatherhead's *Psychology and Life,* I knew very little about psychosomatic medicine. However, I sensed unconsciously that my body had become my best ally and had helped to spring me loose from an inner servitude I could not handle.

I was, nevertheless, not free enough to leave my religious community, and I began to teach in a denominational school, salving my guilt with frequent preaching and a round of religious and denominational activities. For years I retained an uneasy ambivalence. I was a minister and yet I pursued doctoral studies in literature at the university. I was a teacher of English and yet I could not be a free servant of that art. When after a few years I was invited to teach at the university, I justified that sortie into the secular world by arguing that this would allow me to finish my doctoral degree more quickly. I benefited from my university experience and enjoyed the endless dialogue. This was in the Hutchins, Adler, McKeon era at the university, and every text was read and discussed with enormous seriousness. But I could not be free to be an intellectual, not even a Christian intellectual. I carried within me an enormous guilt about being separated from the parish. I felt as the elder brother must have felt if, after the day's work, and just before caving into bed, he read *Playboy*. I was living in a forbidden world. Sooner or later I knew that I had to return to my servitude.

Servant in Peril

My opportunity came with the entry of America into World War II. Fairly early I decided to become a chaplain and to serve the wounded and dying on a distant battlefield. In making this decision (which I did not share with Sally until it was virtually irrevocable), I acted out of the same old unblessed motives which had brought me into the ministry to start with, as well as out of an enormous egotism. By that time we had two sons, whose existence should certainly have justified my staying where I was, but I was bent on saving the world and not on helping Sally care for two children. Just recently I have been going over my wartime correspondence with the two boys, only one of whom was old enough to know what was happening. It breaks my heart to sense the loneliness and rejection in his childishly printed notes. Perhaps at that stage of my development I had to do what I did, but I cannot forgive myself for not being sensitive to what effect my decision had on a very devoted girl and a perceptive child.

What I was seeking during my three-year stint in the chaplaincy became apparent to me one dark night in the approaches to the Siegfried Line. I suppose I had fairly normal desires to prove myself a hero, but on this occasion I became aware of another motive. Let me say at the outset that most of the time I was a very frightened soldier. I did not like war when it became specific in terms of exploding mortar shells and land mines and droning fighter bombers. I usually looked for deep holes and strong walls to protect me from the wrath to come. But on this one afternoon I found myself walking down a road toward the German pill boxes with only one desire: to atone. I was not suicidal. But I saw that I had spent months of preparation and crossed perilous seas because I needed to die, I needed to be spread-eagled on the cross. Nothing short of this would bring me the blessing. I am confident that in part this dark need arose from seeing myself alive in the midst of all the death. But if I ask why I was not free to live when so many people were dying in horrible ways, I must conclude that it was because I needed to repeat the atonement. I needed to die. Fortunately, because I retained a residue of good sense, I let the occasion pass, and extended my death and dying for another twenty years or more.

When the war was over, I returned to the university and continued with my graduate studies. I also taught and became deeply involved in administration. But I knew in my inward self that much as I admired the university and was quickened by the intellectual excitement I found there, the completion of my doctorate would spell the end of the chapter. I was destined to return to the faith community which has figured so largely in my spiritual servitude.

In speaking thus about my relationship to my church I do not want to be judgmental in any way. I have been fortunate above measure to spend most of my life in the company of the kind of people with whom I served. I have already indicated my intellectual and emotional commitment to the faith posture of that church. I need to say that it was only when I returned to the church and its institutions that I became alive and creative. Whereas at the university I found myself getting increasingly defensive and hostile as well as imaginatively sterile, at my denominational college and seminary I felt a kind of rightness and a kind of peace. I now see that the rightness and the peace may have overlaid some deeper hangups, but if they did, that was my problem and not that of the many beautiful people with whom I worked.

Conditions of Servitude

In any event in 1948 I left the university forever and settled down to be a scholar, teacher, and administrator within my denomination. The first eleven years I figuratively toiled for Rachel, for I loved my students and my colleagues and was forced by circumstance to master a range of intellectual disciplines which would not have come within my ken as a free-wheeling academician. For the last six of the eleven years I worked my way into the history of the free religious movements stemming from the Reformation and capped my study with a definitive history of the denomination. My freest year was 1956–57 which I spent in Sweden doing research into the sources of our church life.

But in 1959 my life took another turn. The president of the college and seminary resigned, and I followed him into the job. My feelings about taking the presidency were most ambivalent, a statement which can now be given greater credence than when it was first made. On the one hand I liked the relative freedom of teaching and scholarship, for in it I could escape at least for a time from the more burdensome aspects of my servitude.

On the other hand I was human enough to be challenged by the larger responsibilities, powers, initiatives, and quite honestly the prestige of a position which would make me the head of a complex of three schools and hence thrust me into the top echelon of denominational leadership. The salary and perquisites were also an improvement over those of my teaching position.

However, considerable as the inducements were to accept the presidency of the schools, I do not honestly believe that taken by themselves they would have lured me out of the relative serenity of my academic covert. I knew before I accepted the presidency that in our denomination such a position brought disproportionate anguish. Noncredal in its doctrinal stance, the Covenant Church was a true polyglot of old-line Bible-loving "mission friends" with their emphasis on life in Christ and what Zinzendorf called *Herzenreligion* (heart religion); of neo-Calvinistic fundamentalists attracted from main line churches to those of the Covenant by the assumed biblicism and orthodoxy of the latter; and of a younger more miscellaneous group of ministers and lay people who were in reaction to fundamentalism but had not yet formulated a very positive faith stance of their own.

Because the president of the schools had a seminary for which he was responsible, he was always bobbing around in this boiling brine of denominational controversy. Because he was the head of a denominational college, he had to try to mediate between parents who thought he was too liberal in his stance on student behavior and those who thought he was too conservative, in fact, an old fuddy-duddy. He had to try to please students so that they would recommend the school to other students but not to the extent of alienating the pastors or the lay givers in the church or the major contributors outside the church or the alumni or the business community. If he tried too hard to please the money people, he would worry those faculty members who were chronically suspicious of capitalism, private initiative, the profit motive, etc. And all of this before any suggestion of the SDS, faculty and student governance, Columbia and Kent State.

I mean quite literally that the positive aspects of the school presidency would not have induced me to accept the job if something stronger and deeper and older had not tipped the scales in its favor. What this thing was should be clear from all that has gone before. It was my neurotic need to repeat the atonement, to seek out the place and the circumstance most difficult and perhaps most repugnant to me; to labor without the hope of blessing or celebration; to cut myself off from opportunities in the far country in order to work the fields around the old gray farmhouse; to envy the freedom and the grace of those who impiously and irreverently, yes scandalously, did their own thing and sang their own song.

Hence I took the job and toiled another eleven years for Leah. I would probably still be in it if I had not, some time in the summer of 1967, come face to face with the real me and suddenly discovered the simple but overwhelming fact which I had preached and written about for thirty years—that we are justified by faith alone and not by works, "lest any man should boast." What this meant for *me,* quite practically, was that God had already accepted the real *me* in Christ and that it was O.K. to be that *me.* I did not have to overlay that *me* with any sweat-soaked slave shirt of my own. I did not have to be a professional prelate, preacher, president, pundit, professor, Protestant, or anything else to make it with God. I didn't have to be eaten up by malarial mosquitoes, slog through mud, contract dysentery, translate the Bible, swallow the mutterings and the up-tight rantings of paranoids, study the next move on the great religio-political chessboard, win every argument and every tennis game, speak to 50,000 people, read the Bible through eighteen times, pray for twenty-four hours at a stretch, balance the budget, be listed in *Who's Who,* empty bedpans, bridge the generation gap, be bored, be insulted, be tense, be tired—I did not, praise God in the highest, need to *do* any of these or *be* any of these in order to make it with God. I was free to be me and to be human.

Two Angels

Two angels brought me out of the city. The first was a group of Christian people (including my wife Sally) at Laity Lodge in Texas, who, in the summer of 1967, while I was still functioning as some sort of expert on interpersonal relations, loved me enough to let me be me. This allowed me to see how important it had been for me to be the professional Christian who was chronically expert, bestowed his insights from above, gave directive advice, made most of the important decisions, and kept control of people by outarticulating them and never letting them win an argument.

The second angel was my friend Myron C. Madden, who made the biblical concept of blessing meaningful to me and who, in some very exciting and demanding conversations, led me to see what I am trying to say in this book, namely, that the unblessed son in the Lord's parable is the "good" one: the scrupulous Pharisee, the pious Protestant, the self-appointed martyr, the dedicated Marxist or Maoist or Muslim—the morally constipated, dyspeptic, up-tight good person who has never gone to the party or held a red balloon in his hot little fist. He also helped me to see that I was such a one, that, despite a certain amount of intellectual and verbal freedom, I was locked into the old gray farm and that I really did not believe that the music and dancing and the rustle of new clothes and the smell of roasting veal and especially the glad, loving faces were for me.

I am sure that Myron Madden will hotly disown that he is or ever wanted to be an angel or that he helped me with anything. But despite such beautifully shy disclaimers, he did provide the freedom and the input in the dialogue which made the biblical insights luminous for both of us.

Having thus identified myself with the elder brother, I began to read the New Testament in a new way. And I saw what I had not seen before, that the curse Christ lifted by becoming a curse for us was not just the curse of active sin—boozing and wenching and hating and murdering—but the curse of unfaith and its peculiar kind of goodness; that he died for the thieves and the whores but even more for those who thought they didn't need anybody to die for them. Especially did he die for those who, like myself, had done the theological cop-out and who, because they could discuss learnedly the topics of faith and hope and love and identify with Augustine and Anselm and Francis and C. S. Lewis, did not need to affirm, indeed had no right to affirm, the nail-biting, unsure, sometimes manic little homunculus who lived inside them.

Well, all that changed, not in a moment and the twinkling of an eye, but slowly and painfully over many months. (And, of course, it is still going on.) I began to ask myself, if it is true that Christ has broken into the order of nature and history by which you seemed bound everlastingly to Ixion's wheel, and that he has freed you from the unblessedness of the unblessed so that you need no longer try to make it with anybody but can be truly yourself—if all this is true, as it most assuredly is, what practical, everyday, toast-and-orange-juice meaning does this have for you? And I concluded that the blessing of Christ meant I could hang loose and wait for signals. It meant that within obvious creaturely limitations and commitments I could truly be a pilgrim. It did not mean that I had to leave what I was doing or that anybody had to leave what he was doing, but it meant the freedom to go or to stay.

For reasons, some of which are immaterial to this book, I chose to go. I left the presidency of my college and a whole complex of associations and responsibilities in Chicago, not because I thought any of these things unimportant—which they are not—and not because I did not love the people with whom I lived and worked with a fierce and undying love, but because I was no longer equipped to serve them as I once had. I could no longer be the public, official person who made decisions based largely, although not entirely, on what was good for the institution. I believe in institutions and I cannot conceive of a society without them. I think presidents, and senators, and judges, and board chairmen, and police officers, and all the other tired gray people who keep us from falling apart deserve our gratitude and respect and love. (I sometimes think it might be a very instructive experience for anarchists with a pathological hatred of power to have to face the need of forming a government and collecting the garbage regularly.) But to believe in the need for an Establishment is one thing; to be permanently committed to being an Establishment man is something else again. More and more as I discovered my right to be a person and my freedom from the neurotic servitude I have described, I felt free to do something else and to be something else than I had done and been.

I was helped to my decision by an episode which occurred in the summer of 1969 and which I have described as a "little Damascus." I was in the act of preparing what might be called a *defense* of the educational Establishment. The college I served as president had for years maintained a pietistic concern for student behavior. It did not, like many Christian colleges, limit enrollment to committed Christians, but it tried to keep campus life running within a clearly defined channel. Thus it did not permit smoking on the campus, it required chapel twice a week, and it maintained a taboo on officially sponsored social dancing. It also kept fairly tight control of residence halls, particularly those serving women students. There were clearly stated rules about hours and dormitory visiting. In terms of campus governance, although the administration and faculty were listening to student demands for more participation, as well as freer policies on student publications and off-campus speakers, the rapid growth of student power posed a threat to the campus and particularly to me. I was faced that summer, I felt, with the need of going in the direction of more topside control, a mild form of Hayakawaism, in which, in response to the conservative elements in the denomination and some members of my board, I would follow a tougher line on student power than that advocated by the majority of the faculty and those in the administration responsible for student affairs. The time was ripe, I thought, for taking a position and fighting a major battle in which *we,* that is, the Establishment, would reclaim the initiative from *them,* that is, the students, and return the school to some sort of traditional stability.

But while I was in the process of working out the defense of the Establishment, I found myself more and more in sympathy with the students. I began to understand the psychological and spiritual rootage from which they came; better than that I began to *feel* it. I sensed that the impatience, the carping, the cynicism, the pressure, even the threat of violence on the part of students, were the outgrowth of a basic idealism, misguided perhaps and often uninformed and naïve, but more honest and real than that which motivated me. I was in the process of delivering my defense of the Establishment when I suddenly saw that, like another Establishment man, Saul of Tarsus, I was consenting to the death of people whom I did not understand and whose relation to the mysterious processes of history I had chosen to ignore.

I was not immediately converted. Like Saul, I have gone through a process of blinding and partial seeing and some confused signals. But after my little Damascus I could never again so univocally polarize myself with the Establishment and against student power, black power, woman power, and whatever other minority manifestation I was to face.

Because of my little Damascus in the summer of 1969, I was persuaded to look at students as people, as persons. Just as I had been or was being delivered from the professional cocoon which had been wrapped around me, so I felt the need to divest students of the stereotype "students," and in my thinking and feeling, at least, let them function as people. The result was that my last year in the presidency was characterized by a closer and more sympathetic relationship to students and, I hope, faculty, than I had ever had.

But this new feeling about students probably served to disqualify me as president of a denominational school. Many supporters of the school felt, I think rightly, that I had gone soft and could no longer be trusted to guide the ship or control either crew or passengers. But right or wrong in their judgment, I had the freedom to leave. I took farewell forever of a school I love and of the work of a lifetime. But more germane to my thesis, I said good-bye to an old compulsion. I buried the elder brother out in the fields, washed, changed my clothes, oiled my hair and beard, and entered my Father's house. And there was music and dancing.

Chapter 3

The
Sons
of
Perdition

To be unblessed is to be a believer, a strenuous pilgrim spirit stretching forever toward an elusive rest. To be unblessed is to be a moral *Streber*,* a mountain climber, a prophet, an ascetic, a good girl or boy, a dutiful, anxious, compulsive, clean, orderly, thrifty person who straightens pictures and uses a strong mouthwash.

To be unblessed may also be to fall from belief into doubt, and from duty into cynicism. It may be to stop hoping and to descend into despair. It may be to turn political, not in the manner of the glad arranger who is secure enough to make things better for everybody, but in the insecure, suspicious manner of a Machiavelli.

Judas Iscariot fits the picture of the despairing unblessed. A great deal of both charitable and uncharitable ink has been

* German, a social climber.

spilled over Judas. He has been called a habitual thief, a disappointed revolutionary, a misguided idealist. I shall not presume to add to the confusion by suggesting an adequate motive. In some ways Judas may have been mastered by Iago's "motiveless malignity."

But if we are going to talk about motives, Judas seems more the victim of envy than of frustration and his treachery more a crime of passion than of blocked ambition. John calls Judas a thief, and we are told that he was given thirty pieces of silver for his dark deed, but among the motives greed is hardly a serious candidate. Judas acts more like a disappointed lover than a man who lusts for money or sees his dream of power dissolve into nothingness.

The twelve disciples of Jesus are pictured in the synoptic Gospels as sharing intimately in his life and teaching, but in actual fact we know very little about them as a group. Even the lists do not exactly jibe. Matthew and Mark mention a Thaddaeus whose name is not in Luke's list, and Luke has a Judas (not Iscariot) missing from Matthew and Mark. John's list of disciples is even more puzzling. He mentions by name only Andrew, Peter, Philip, Thomas, Judas Iscariot, and Nathanael (unknown to the synoptics). The sons of Zebedee do not occur in chapters 1–20 but are mentioned in chapter 21, which seems, without any reflection on its authenticity, a puzzling appendix to the rest of the Gospel. John, one of the sons of Zebedee and the traditional writer of the Gospel of John, is never mentioned by name in the Gospel. He is thought to be the person referred to as "the disciple whom Jesus loved."

In the synoptic Gospels and in John, references to Judas Iscariot are clustered at the end of Jesus' life, and we know almost nothing of the role he played in the daily life of the disciples, except that he seems to have been the team treasurer. John says of him, "and as he had the money box he used to take what was put into it" (John 12:6, RSV). There is another reference to Judas's money box in John 13:29.

In the synoptics, three of the disciples, Peter and the two sons of Zebedee (James and John), seem to constitute an inner circle. It is this group which accompanies Jesus to the Mount of Transfiguration and into the depths of the Garden of Gethsemane. That the three occupied a special place is indicated by Jesus' obvious dependence on Peter throughout the Gospels and by the request of the mother of the sons of Zebedee that James and John be allowed to sit on the right and left hand of Jesus in his kingdom.* Peter and John are the disciples chosen by Jesus to make arrangements for the Passover.

In John's Gospel, as indicated, there is no reference to the sons of Zebedee in chapters 1–20. But if the Beloved Disciple is indeed John, Peter and John figure prominently in the closing chapters of the narrative. Jesus washes Peter's feet; John lies next to Jesus at the Supper; John and Peter converse about the betrayal; Peter and another disciple "known to the high priest" follow Jesus to Annas and Caiaphas; John stands at the foot of the cross; Peter and John see the empty tomb; in the postresurrection appearance at the Sea of Tiberias, both Peter and John are central.

On the basis of available evidence, we must conclude that the prominence of Peter and John in the four Gospels was a historic fact and not something read back into the narratives

---

* In Mark 10:35–41 the two disciples make the request for themselves. In Luke 22:24–27 the dispute is shifted to the upper room. In John 13:1–20 the controversy is only implied and becomes the occasion for the foot-washing.

to strengthen the position of the two men in their respective church communities. If so, we may have a clue to the turmoil of feeling in Judas which led to the betrayal.

In order to set the stage further, let us review briefly the circumstances in the upper room as they are given to us by the four evangelists. In all of the accounts, the betrayal of Judas plays a prominent part. And in all of them Jesus' word about the sign of betrayal seems to suggest that Judas was placed near him at the table.

Matthew writes:

> As they were eating, he said, "Truly, I say to you, one of you will betray me." And they were very sorrowful, and began to say to him one after another, "Is it I, Lord?" He answered, "He who has dipped his hand in the dish with me, will betray me. . . ." Judas, who betrayed him, said, "Is it I, Master?" He said to him, "You have said so" (Matt. 26:21–25, RSV).

Mark writes:

> Jesus said, "Truly, I say to you, one of you will betray me, one who is eating with me." They began to be sorrowful, and to say to him one after another, "Is it I?" He said to them, "It is one of the twelve, one who is dipping bread in the same dish with me" (Mark 14:18–20, RSV).

Luke writes:

> "But behold the hand of him who betrays me is with me on the table. . . ." And they began to question one another, which of them it was that would do this (Luke 22:21,23, RSV).

John writes:

> ". . . it is that the scripture may be fulfilled, 'He who ate my bread has lifted his heel against me.' . . ."
> When Jesus had thus spoken, he was troubled in spirit, and

testified, "Truly, truly, I say to you, one of you will betray me."
The disciples looked at one another, uncertain of whom he spoke.
One of his disciples, whom Jesus loved, was lying close to the
breast of Jesus; so Simon Peter beckoned to him and said, "Tell
us who it is of whom he speaks." So lying thus, close to the breast
of Jesus, he said to him, "Lord, who is it?" Jesus answered, "It is
he to whom I shall give this morsel when I have dipped it." So
when he had dipped the morsel, he gave it to Judas, the son of
Simon Iscariot. Then after the morsel, Satan entered into him.
Jesus said to him, "What you are going to do, do quickly." Now
no one at the table knew why he said this to him. Some thought
that, because Judas had the money box, Jesus was telling him,
"Buy what we need for the feast"; or, that he should give something to the poor. So, after receiving the morsel, he immediately
went out; and it was night (John 13:18,21–30, RSV).

It is true that the statements in Matthew, Mark, and Luke—
"He who has dipped his hand in the dish with me," "one who
is dipping bread in the same dish with me," "the hand of him
who betrays me is with me on the table"—may simply mean
that the betrayer is one of the table guests. According to the
custom, the dip of bitter herb sauce was a common dish. But
it is hard to understand why Jesus would make the designation
of the traitor so general. He has already said that one of them
would betray him. Why would he simply repeat the statement
in another form?

The Gospel of John seems to give us the answer. Judas was
placed close to Jesus. Let us have a recognized authority on the
Gospel of John, Dr. Wilbert F. Howard, describe the scene:

The Oriental custom was to recline on a couch, with the left arm
resting on a cushion upon the table and the right arm free. Sometimes two reclined on the same divan; the one on the right would
have his back turned to his neighbor, with his head resting at the
level of his neighbor's breast. That was the position of the Beloved
Disciple. Where was Peter placed? It is often assumed that he

would lie in the place of honor above Jesus, i.e. on his left. But in that case his communication with the Beloved Disciple would be extremely difficult, and *it is more likely that Judas occupied that place.* This would explain the action in vs. 26 and the whispered words in vs. 27b. Probably Peter was on the right of the Beloved Disciple. If he was reclining on another divan, we can more easily account for the signal as well as for the whispered appeal.[1]

If Dr. Howard is right, and Judas did occupy the place of honor at the table, we are confronted with a tragic irony. For then, at the feast of betrayal, Judas symbolically occupies the place he has long coveted in relation to Jesus and never could secure.

If the theory of the "blessed" and "unblessed child" has any validity, Judas may represent a person who, having never made it with his father, is locked into the need of making it with someone who has gained his admiration and love—a substitute parent figure. If Judas was unblessed in this sense, his contact with Jesus could well have resulted in growing attraction and even adoration of our Lord. Judas needed to "make it" with Jesus. Perhaps his acceptance of the treasurer's chores was not so much the result of his greed as his compulsion to serve. Like unblessed people in general, Judas may have spent so much time trying to please Jesus that he never really was himself. Hence he never entered into the freedom and blessedness of just being Judas and of letting Jesus give him whatever station or assignment was appropriate for him. Instead Judas, motivated by his love for Jesus and his need to be important for Jesus, developed a pathological envy toward all those who came between him and his master. His grumbling about the wasted perfume in the house of Lazarus would then not be the result of greed but of jealousy, and his ultimate betrayal of

Jesus would spring not from frustrated political ambition, but from the realization that he would never make it with Jesus in the way that Peter and John had made it. He would be beloved, but not in the way John was beloved. He would be trusted or mistrusted, but not in the way Peter was trusted or mistrusted. And so he took the route of scorned lovers; he destroyed the very person he loved most. Without any suggestion of inversion, Judas may have murdered Jesus with the same motive as impelled Othello to strangle Desdemona. For the unblessed, it is intolerable to be number two. Judas did not understand that in Jesus' company everyone is ultimately number one, but Judas couldn't wait.

If the motive of Judas was indeed envy—that is, the refusal to accept his identity and the smoldering desire to be someone else, if in that way he might get closer to Jesus—we may have to exchange envy for pride as the root sin. For whereas pride unduly enlarges the ego and breathes into it the desire to be equal with God, envy denies the ego in a bad way and ultimately destroys it. Judas betrays Jesus because he has first of all betrayed himself; it is a murdered not an inflated ego which hands Jesus over to his assassins and which finally hangs from the tree of malediction.

The same kind of demonic disenchantment works not only in individuals but in societies.

The world is full of disenchantment and accommodation—the politics of despair. If you are unblessed, make the world work without a blessing. Cosimo de Medici, the Renaissance prince, says, "You follow infinite objects, I finite ones. You place your ladders in the heavens and I on earth that I may not seek so high or fall so low." [2] The incredible dreariness of technological, bureaucratic society which is a kind of freezing of the processes of life and history (that is, an elimination of their risks) reflects the loss of hope in the blessing. People who know that they will never make it to heaven establish an uneasy truce with earth. There is, hence, in the demeanor of the politician, the bureaucrat, the social engineer, the technologist, the unionizer, and the logical industrialist (who no longer gambles) an icy despair. He is like Mammon in Milton's Hell who counsels the devils to make the best of a bad situation.

> Our greatness will appear
> Then most conspicuous when great things of small,
> Useful of hurtful, prosperous of adverse
> We can create, and in what place so e'er
> Thrive under evil, and work ease out of pain
> Through labour and endurance.[3]

In this connection it is inviting to think of totalitarian societies with their barracks civilization as accommodations to despair. They have sought by a desperate atheism to eliminate once and for all the indignity of election. God shall have no favorites! Pasternak's *Doctor Zhivago* and Solzhenitsyn's *The First Circle* reflect the horror of a society in which all hope is abandoned. It is significant that for Solzhenitsyn contemporary Russia is the first circle of Dante's Hell, that is Limbo, where there is no physical suffering—only a pervasive hopelessness.

The unblessed has available to him a final act which, in Augustine's words, is a "darkened shadow of omnipotence." He can make an assault on God by trying to destroy his creation. Lucifer does his thing by seducing Adam and Eve, Judas by betraying Christ, Hitler by his assault on the Jews, successions of Stalinist politicians by diverse outrages. Much of the same sort of destructiveness is reflected in the language of some contemporary militants. If they cannot achieve a better day for their people, they want to pull down the house on everyone's head and take their enemies with them to destruction.

But this final desperate act is evidence that, even for the hopeless, blessing has a substantial quality and that election to blessedness is real. The rage which manifests itself in death and destruction is not motivated merely by the lack of the essentials of physical life—food, clothing, housing—but by the conviction that one has been passed by in favor of someone else. "Jacob have I loved, but Esau have I hated."

Such destruction is, in the last analysis, suicidal, and it is no accident that Judas's final act is to hang himself. What this tells us is that politics is not only a response to the despair of unblessedness. It generates its own despair and increases the distance between the blesser and the unblessed. Cain goes out looking for death, and all his sad kin—Ishmael, Esau, and the legendary lost tribes—move restlessly across the face of the earth savoring the bitterness of being unchosen.

Chapter 4

Birthrights
and
Heirlooms

Chosenness or blessing is clearly illustrated in the transmission of things from one generation to another. The opening of the will figures in a number of literary works, but the dynamism of the testamentary act in its relation to parental favor is seldom given full justice.

Now the fact is that very little feeling adheres to the distribution of such measurable and divisible things as money, securities, land. Surviving heirs usually manage to horse-trade in such a way as to arrive at acceptable conclusions. Where things can be shared and shared alike problems can be solved amicably.

The situation is entirely different if the heirloom is encrusted with sentiment and if the giving of it is interpreted as a sign of blessing. The blessing cannot be divided and neither can the birthright. Families have been split over things with almost no intrinsic value: a goat hair rug, an old clock, a desk, a picture, a soup tureen, a cutaway coat, an old wedding gown, a buggy wheel.

Let us look at a few cases. A family of several children, of which the oldest is a daughter, has one heirloom—a Sèvres figurine which, though chipped and repaired, is still of great value to the family. An unwritten law stipulates that the object pass to the oldest child and from that child to his or her oldest. The daughter, though married, has no children of her own and decides that the figurine should be given back to the family. But to whom? The next child in line is a brother, but before he can receive the figurine, he dies. Now the next child in line, also a brother, has a claim to the object, but his right is challenged by the oldest son of the older brother. The upshot of this controversy is a hopelessly divided family.

Logical people who have no Sèvres figurine to fight about look at this internecine struggle as stupid, vicious, wasteful, and even ludicrous. A search through antiquarian shops would in a short time uncover a flawless figurine at a manageable price and the bloodshed could be avoided. So goes the reasoning. But it is not *a* figurine that is desired; it is *the* figurine.

Why is this so? Probably because it is a symbol of the family's birthright. It is soaked in the preference of the parents and carries with it, almost like an animistic fetish, the peculiar favor of the tribe. The one who ends up with the figurine has the mana. In a special way he is in.

In another family the sacred object is an Afghanistani prayer rug, undistinguished in color and without any special merit. But it is watched with intense interest by all members of the family. When it is removed for cleaning, each child suspects that it has been given to one of the others. I have been told that when the last day comes and the rug has to be given to someone, the fur will really fly.

In still another family the object is a rocking chair. In that chair great-great-grandmother Higginbottom knit the socks worn by great-grandfather at the Second Battle of Bull Run. For over a hundred years the Higginbottoms have been buzzing angrily around the chair. The lucky recipients are always nonchalant about it. "That old thing—who wants it?" "We took it because no one else wanted it." Or frequently, "We are the only ones in the family who really know anything about antiques or really care for them."

The blessed child or children have a fairly consistent attitude about the birthright. Like Jacob, they want the whole hog— the undivided thing. They consequently resist an equitable sharing which seems to them a violation of a natural right.

This presumption rests upon something very ancient and very profound—the conviction that the favored child possesses not only his parents' favor but a sizable share of the world he inhabits. That is, the favor is not only familial but general.

Part II

THE
FAMILY
OF
BLESSING

~THE LAST
AND LASTING
PARTY~

| Chapter 5 | God's Identity and Mine |

I have spoken earlier of the two an-
gels who brought me out of the city: a new acceptance of myself, and a new understanding of the biblical doctrine of
blessing, to which I was helped by my friend Myron Madden.
I would now like to put these things in a larger context. I
would like to show how insights from relational philosophy
and psychology harmonize with the major tenets of Christian
doctrine; I would also like to show how the traditional church
has dealt with its heritage of blessing; finally, although not in
a systematic way, I would like to suggest what the emerging
church can look like when it accepts the gift of celebration and
is free to go to the party.

In attempting to do this I will no doubt sound as moralistic
and sermonizing as some of the people from whom I differ.
If so, I'll have to confess the sin and ask for forgiveness. For
what we need is not so much effort and discipline as a clearer

vision of what has already been revealed. We need to see what we can be and where we can go or perhaps what we already are and where we already are if we will only rub the sleep out of our eyes.

Faith and the Relational

What do I mean by harmonizing relational psychology and Christian doctrine? Am I not, for whatever reason, seeking to rationalize my adherence to an ancient body of beliefs? Some time ago, a woman who had read an article of mine in *Faith at Work* (April 1971), entitled "It's All Right to Be Merely Human," wrote to me:

> I am not sure I understand the process by which your acceptance of yourself happened. What I am saying is—did God play a part at all? Reread your article and eliminate every reference to God. Couldn't you have found this way for yourself by allowing your humanness to surface because it occurred to you that to submerge it was stupid and a poor use of energy?

What this lady is really asking is: why do you need God to be yourself, to be human, and to be relatable? I am not sure that I can answer this question for anybody but myself. And I am not sure that my personal answer will satisfy her or anyone else. But I want to try to answer it for myself.

In the first place, whatever the theoretical possibilities, the practical experience seems to be that encounter, sensitivity, and marathon groups, though starting from secular assumptions, often move toward some sort of theological or religious framework. The personal and relational experience seems to need the support of overarching meaning. This meaning is often only implied or is stated so vaguely that it cannot be identified with any known system of beliefs. It may sound like Yoga or

Freud, but it is unmistakably there, and what it seems to say is that the design of the universe makes personhood and relationship (love) better than unpersonhood and isolation. It also seems to say that fixing or freezing humanity into any superhuman pattern is unhealthy.

I accept the validity of the conclusions, but I am troubled by the vagueness of some of the assumptions on which the conclusions rest. For me, at least, Christian insight fits the facts of existence better than the beliefs of the secularist-humanists.* Much in the Christian faith not only parallels contemporary relational thinking but actually deepens and strengthens it. Christian theology, when it is freed from some of its barnacles, provides unique solutions for many of the deep problems arising from our life together. And the Christian life style, when it is unpretentious and truly dumb and scared, can bring a new dimension to personal and communal life.

But beyond the "fitness" of Christian truth for me, I must confess to the ongoing need of the Christian God to try to keep me honest and on course. For no matter how attractive a fresh insight about human nature may be to me or how inviting openness and love may seem, I am a curiously warped creature who keeps warping existence.

This was brought home to me forcibly a few weeks ago. I

---

* In saying this I hope I am not venting any theological bile on the humanistic advocates of sensitivity and encounter who do not share my faith. It is useful to observe that thousands of up-tight Christians have been transformed by such relational processes into living and breathing human beings. It is painful, but true, that the institutional church has often reinforced sick attitudes and behavior in its members, not because such unhealth is intrinsic to Christian faith and life, but because unhealed people have twisted the faith to meet their own needs. If, in fact, I had to judge secular-humanist encounter groups and conventional Christian churches by the sole criterion of concern for personhood and relationship, I might have to conclude that the seculars are winning by a wide margin.

had been off to a week-long conference in which I was separated from my immediate family. I was hence freed from the ordinary frustrations which trouble home life: bathroom priorities, sleeping habits, working patterns, and other things. I was by myself and for myself, like a monk in a luxurious cell. I was hence freer to be a person for people—a man for others— and I became increasingly pleased with my self-transcendence. I seemed calm, energetic, devoted, free. I was great.

Then I flew home and landed splash in the family kin-kith duck-pond. There were commitments, decisions, promises, chores imposed on me. There was, in other words, a fabric of history—a before and after. Because by the circumstances of blood and marriage, I was accountable to people—and, Lord, how many people!—I was no longer free to choose my course of action. It was chosen for me. I was no longer a volunteer; I was a draftee. I was no longer a swan flying whitely against the blue sky. I was an ordinary domestic duck paddling around grayly with other ducks. And I didn't like my duck image at all.

This experience has helped me to see that without God to support, judge, redeem, restore, heal, enable, and fulfill me in the midst of my moral life and not in some attractive fantasy, I shall never get to the party and enter into the joy of the Lord. I shall try to explain what this means to me in the pages that follow. I am not sure that it is a valid argument, but I think it is an honest confession. And that is all it is meant to be.

The Maker of My Identity

One of the main doctrines of the Christian faith is that God is the maker of heaven and earth. This means not only that he created the stuff out of which separate things were made but that he formed each thing and gave each a distinct identity.

God can give each thing its identity because he has an identity. He is not a generally distributed gas; he is personal. He is identified with our history; he is the God of Abraham, Isaac, and Jacob and, in a special way, the father of our Lord. Jesus says, "he who has seen me has seen the Father" (John 14:9, RSV), and Paul writes that we see "the glory of God in the face of Jesus Christ" (2 Cor. 4:6). The God who made the world is thus not only the "ground of being" but a personal being we can know, particularly because he has revealed himself in Jesus.

The identity of God lays the foundation for the all-rightness of my own identity. That God is personal allows me to believe not only that I am a person, or at least have the capacity to become a person, but that my personhood matters to him who made me. My "I" is ultimately important because as an "I" or a "thou" I can relate to the I-ness and Thou-ness of God. When I cry, he hears me; when he speaks, I can answer.

That God has established my identity, not as a thing but in analogy to his own identity, means that both he and I are responsible for me. He has responsibility for me both in the sense that he guarantees my freedom and in the sense that he underwrites all the processes of growth and decay. I can actualize my identity—become my "I," my me—and use my gifts, or I can splinter the me and abuse my gifts. I can follow many roads to heaven or to hell. But whichever way I go, he knows about it. He has been there before me. All roads are his. Even when, as in Romans 1, God gives me up, my given-upness is within the perimeter of his will. This is the meaning of Dante's great insight in the *Inferno* that even Hell does not bring man outside God's orbit. The kingdom of desolation has the inscription over its gate:

> *Justice* moved my great maker; God eternal
> Wrought me: the *power,* and the unsearchably
> High *wisdom,* and the primal *love* supernal.[1]

What this says is that there is no point in my pilgrimage which is outside of God's ordinance and hence devoid of meaning. There is no hole through which I can fall into meaninglessness. "If I make my bed in Sheol, thou art there!" (Ps. 139:8, RSV).

But the God who has established my identity and the cosmos it occupies has left me free to go in any direction. The song "I want to be me, I want to be free" is, as far as it goes, the situation into which we have been created. The bondages which have been imposed on my me-ness or freeness are not of God's making. They have been forged by people and by circumstances and most probably by myself.

To have my identity established by God means that I have the freedom and security to choose. I have the freedom and security to sin. I can eat all the lawful fruit in the garden and I can eat the forbidden fruit. I can freely adore him who is the source of my freedom but I also have the opportunity to challenge him, to try to make myself the center of existence and to render absolute my me-ness and my freeness. Augustine speaks of a mimicked liberty "to do those things unpermitted me, a darkened likeness of Thy omnipotency."[2] I have such liberty.

Identity and Goodness

My me-ness, my personhood, is given substance by relationships. I become accountable to God and to others. I am my brother's keeper. I also become accountable for things and to things. I am set down in the garden "to till and keep it." So I

am a keeper. I am a groundskeeper and housekeeper and bee-
keeper. I am responsible for a slice of life. I am a steward.
All this gives me body. I become what is called a "good"
person, a "solid citizen." I know who I am. Because I have a
responsibility for my own life and the life of others, I conserve
things, mix my labor with them, cause them to multiply, and
use them wisely. I become the adequate or good man or
woman.

Proverbs 31:10–31 gives us a beautiful description of a good
wife. With a few changes this passage could apply to any adequate person, man or woman. The good wife knows who she
is and accepts responsibility for life around her. She works
diligently and purposefully; she is a shrewd buyer; she provides well for her family and is not unmindful of the poor;
she is strong and dignified but without any semblance of vanity or false charm.

To be thus adequate seems to be the *summum bonum* of
life.* The first Psalm talks about the good man as a tree planted
by the water. He is rooted. To be thus rooted is to be reverent
toward life and to cherish the fabrics which keep it orderly.
It is to love the Law. It is to have regard for the ceremonial
and dutiful, the traditional and consistent. It is to like order
and to like to order. To be rooted, reverential, and orderly is
also to see the end from the beginning and to program out
disorder. It is to be impatient with those who live in chaos and
to label them "chaff which the wind drives away" (Ps. 1:4).†

* Aristotle speaks of happiness as "an activity of the soul in accordance
with virtue." *Nichomachean Ethics,* trans. W. D. Ross (New York:
Oxford University Press, 1942), p. 1102a.
† A contemporary Brazilian novel by Jorge Amado, *Doña Flor and
Her Two Husbands* (New York: Bantam Books, 1971), presents the
second of the husbands as this sort of good, reliable person. The first
husband is, appropriately, volcanic, prodigal, irresponsible—chaff.

73

Because life is so risky and disorder so costly to the community, the good man is respected and his example is held up as worthy of emulation. He becomes a model. Classical literature is filled with the exploits of noble men and women, and the education of children through the centuries has been focused on heroic people whose behavior was above and beyond the call of duty.

Since we live near Washington, it is our privilege now and then to drive our guests over to the capital for a typical tourist look-see. It has struck me lately that for the visitor the city is mostly a vast outdoor Westminster Abbey in which the monuments of the noble dead have become objects of pilgrimage and devotion. The size and splendor of the monuments are superhuman. They remind us of the vast solemn faces in Egyptian temples which represent not only some dead king but a god-king or king-god. Lincoln, whose angular, awkward presence and homely face were thought by his contemporaries to be pure "hicksville," has become an overpowering marble Pharaoh. And the words of J. F. Kennedy, once the hot, idealistic sentiments of a boy president breathed out over a cold, torpid nation, have become almost pretentious in marble. It is impossible to read them in their present setting and to believe that Kennedy was not a demigod but a human male with back trouble and a shaky marriage.

It is not my intent to derogate goodness. God has made the world and me in such a way that we can only survive if we keep house and husband our resources. "The law," as Paul says, "is holy" (Rom. 7:12). This means that I can't escape the burden of cultivating my garden. To be me means to be integrated—to be good. It means to learn my lessons, wipe my feet, wash behind my ears, and do a thousand other things which life in community requires me to do. It probably also means to do these things as well as I can.

But if that is so, what is wrong with striving for adequacy, or what goes wrong with it? I am seized at this point by a vast uneasiness and certainly by embarrassment. For how can I talk sensibly about both the necessity of being good in order to be me and the terrible hazard of goodness? In what sense is the order of things both holy and the energy of sin (1 Cor. 15:56).

After I had given my witness in a Midwestern church recently, a young girl came to me genuinely puzzled. "You say that it is O.K. to be me," she said, "and I really want to be me, but I am not satisfied with the me I am. What can I do?" I didn't have a very good answer. What I think she was saying was that as a high school student she was being encouraged to be a *better* student and was provided with models of educational and social adequacy; in church she was being pushed toward being a *better* Christian; at home she was faced with the responsibility of helping to keep house and of being a *better* citizen. In the midst of all this she wanted to run away and to be truly herself. She wanted to assert her selfhood. But she was aware that if she did her own thing, she would probably feel guilty about it. She had been carefully taught that she needed to be better and better.

And, of course, she needed to be. I have a lot of sympathy with the young people who can no longer face the pressure to improve and who drift together in unbusy beehives of self-pity. They have been asked to adopt uncritically the "Protestant ethic" of work, achievement, and thrift by emotionally remote and often hypocritical middle-class parents, and they can't hack it. They want out. So, all right.

But acting on their desire, some of them fail to realize that, entirely apart from their parents, they will have to develop habits and disciplines to band the staves of their personhood. To be themselves they will have to be "good" in some sense. Kicking the slats out of the crib prepares you ultimately to kick the slats out of the crib and not much more.

But kicking the slats out of the crib is not the ultimate sin. Satan and Adam are sometimes presented as young revolutionaries who assert their right to be free in the face of the cosmic establishment. They are praised because, like Prometheus, they dare to rebel against authority. People with a relatively muddy understanding of biblical faith see in Lucifer and in our first parents the promise of the romantic rebels—Blake and Byron, Shelley and Nietzsche.

But if I understand the Bible, the actions of Lucifer and Adam are not so much efforts to rip the fabric of tyranny as to out-god God. Eve's sin, which in Milton's *Paradise Lost* is made to seem the triumph of inflamed sensuality over right reason, looks in the biblical account like an overkill of virtue and common sense. Eve is a farm wife using her head. Here is a fruit that is usable and looks tasteful. It will also improve her understanding. So why not? She eats and she gives it to her husband. And he, being used to her housewifery, accepts the food from her and eats it. The sin is a sort of farm sin. You do everything you have done before except now you think you have it made. You really are the lord of the orchard or the 160 acres. "You have all the good things" (Luke 12:19, TEV).

No, the ultimate sin is not kicking the slats out of the crib. It is thinking ourselves adequate. Nowhere does our independence of God glow so fiercely as in our goodness. When our desire for perfection drives us into moral scrupulousness or even into self-effacing benevolence, we feel with Milton's Eve "divinity within us breeding wings."

This is why ordinary people feel more uneasy about saints, martyrs, and heroes than about sinners, traitors, and cowards. It is very trying to have a saint in for dinner, especially a saint working on being still more saintly. Our guilt may cause us to raise pedestals for spiritual giants and prayer warriors, but we would rather have them gracing our sanctuaries than invading our houses.

It is sometimes argued that we dislike not the seriously but the hypocritically good, but I wonder if the argument holds. The hypocrite like Shakespeare's Malvolio or Molière's Tartuffe may amuse us or even anger us, but the professional holy man depresses us. He is fooling himself in trying to be more than he can be. The self-consciously humble turns out to be proud; the self-consciously chaste woman comes off a prude; the good child is often an intolerable prig.

A classical example of this kind of effort is Benjamin Franklin's "bold and arduous project of arriving at moral perfection" which he writes about in his *Autobiography*. We recall that Franklin, the tireless projector and innovator, asked himself why it should not be possible for him "to live without committing any fault at any time." He consequently developed a scheme for mastering thirteen of the major virtues, including, of all things, humility, in which he hoped to imitate Jesus and Socrates. Needless to say Franklin did not succeed with his project. He is charming when he talks about his failures. For example, he could never master the virtue of order and had to admit himself "incorrigible" in this area. His conclusion is significant: "something, that pretended to be reason, was every now and then suggesting to me that such extreme nicety as I exacted of myself might be a kind of foppery in morals, which,

77

if it were known, would make me ridiculous; that a perfect character might be attended with the inconvenience of being envied and hated, and that a benevolent man should allow a few faults in himself to keep his friends in countenance." [3]

Franklin's honesty serves to rescue this discussion from pompousness, but like most essays on goodness, it leaves us strangely ill at ease. We don't quite trust the moralist whatever we may think of his moral doctrine. We recall Tom Jones's tutor, the philosopher Square in Fielding's novel, who, shortly after having lectured Tom on his romance with Molly Seagrim, is himself found in a most compromising situation in Molly's garret bedroom. Fielding interprets our feelings:

> Philosophers are composed of flesh and blood as well as other human creatures; and however sublimated and refined the theory of these may be, a little practical frailty is as incident to them as to other mortals. It is, indeed, in theory only, and not in practice, as we have before hinted, that consists the difference: for though such great beings think much better and more wisely, they always act exactly like other men. They *know* very well how to subdue all appetites and passions, and to despise both pain and pleasure; and this *knowledge* affords much delightful contemplation, and is easily acquired; but the practice would be vexatious and troublesome; and, therefore, the same wisdom which teaches them to *know* this, teaches them to avoid carrying it into execution [italics mine].[4]

Why is it that we find ourselves agreeing with Fielding's criticism of the moral philosopher and enjoying perhaps too much the discomfiture of Square? Is it that good people show up our evil and activate our guilt? I am sure that this is part of the answer. I am confident that in his caricatures of Methodists, Anglican priests like Thwackum, and moralists like Square, Fielding is defending himself and his style of life.

Nothing can so manipulate our life and ultimately tyrannize it as the person or moral axiom which gets at our guilt.

But this is only part of the answer. The other part is that people of whatever stripe who assume the stance of goodness and moral authority are hiding something not only from us but from themselves. Paul tells it like it is:

> Do you, my friend, pass judgment on others? You have no excuse at all, whoever you are. For when you judge others, but do the same things that they do, you condemn yourself. . . . But you, my friend, do these very things yourself for which you pass judgment on others. Do you think you will escape God's judgment? (Rom. 2:1–3, TEV).

We conclude that the person (or society) who presumes to be morally adequate is, in effect, practicing self-deception and living a lie.

The Sin of Concealment

Bruce Larson has helped me to see that biblical transgressors sin not so much in their active sins as in their refusal to see and to confess what they are. Adam hides himself in the trees of the garden; Cain lies about the murder of his brother; David commits adultery with the wife of one of his valiant men and then tries to cover up that act by murder. It is the compounded lies of Ananias and Sapphira and not their reluctance to share their goods with the Jerusalem commune which bring judgment on them (Acts 5:1–11). Such concealment says that I am not really accountable to anybody for what I do; I live like a god above the judgment of others.

Thus, although the sentiment "I want to be me, I want to be free," is good as far as it goes, it needs a serious qualification. For I cannot want to be so free as to lie about myself to myself. When this happens, the gift given me in creation (the image of God) becomes the occasion for my fall. Hence no matter how much I may rejoice in my identity and in the gifts with which I have been endowed, I need more than myself. When I am in the process of developing my gifts and moving toward adequacy and seizing control over people and situations, I am especially tempted to think that I am more than I am.

The adequate man seeks to be adequate for everything and everybody. He takes Nietzsche's illusion of the Superman seriously. But to try to be superhuman may merely result in our becoming subhuman or inhuman or dehumanized.

The question plagues us: how can we be just human? How can we resist the temptation of Eden to become as gods and live forever? How can we avoid playing the God game and insisting that we are right on all issues?

In Edwin Arlington Robinson's *Nicodemus,* the high priest Caiaphas has a conversation with Nicodemus about Jesus. He states the case for many righteous people:

> "Am I right?
> Why, surely, I am right. I am always right.
> If I were wrong, I should not be a priest." [5]

When we see the arrogance of professional holiness thus unmasked, we react instinctively. If this is what goodness looks like, forget it. But in all seriousness, are we not infected with the same need to be invulnerable, to be right?

But suppose we don't want to be like that, then what do we do? Is there a way out? In order to answer the question, we step back briefly into the world of the Old Testament. In that amazing chronicle of God's acts through the centuries, it is apparent that there are two kinds of people—those who bring gifts to God in order to secure his blessing and those who adore him because they are already secure in his blessing.

The latter—the men and women of blessing—seem to us to be human. That is, they seem to suffer least from the need to prove themselves. Abraham, Moses, David, Job, and some of the unnamed psalmists breathe an air of confidence and trust. They are, to be sure, brooders and worriers, they protest hoarsely to the Most High about the state of the universe and their own feelings and the treachery of other men, they falter and fail and transgress, but they are never out of contact with God. "Though he slay me, yet will I trust in him," Job says in the midst of suffering. They know who they are and they do not confuse their identity with that of the Lord. They howl with pain, but now and then they truly rejoice, like David whirling and leaping before the Ark of God.

We ask wistfully, why not be like that?

But these people of the Old Testament, great as they are, do not exist to be imitated. They shine like points of light in the great darkness, but they cannot give us their light. They prepare the way, but they are not the way. Around them people remain angry and unblessed, like the hairy sons of Jacob before the darling Joseph. They can share in Joseph's grain and hospitality, as later in Egypt, but they cannot share his blessing.

This is not to deny the reality of the blessing or its power. Around the blessed people there grows up a culture of effort.

> Who shall ascend the hill of the Lord?
>   And who shall stand in his holy place?
> He who has clean hands and a pure heart,
>   who does not lift up his soul to what is false,
>   and does not swear deceitfully.
> He will receive blessing from the Lord,

> and vindication from the God of his salvation.
> —Ps. 24:3-5, RSV.

Therefore, let us scrub our hands, purge our hearts, and straighten out our ethics. Let us be supergood.

The Law is received, studied, interpreted. It is given body by instances. Do this, do that. Do not do this. It creates a people of fantastic single-mindedness. Despite apostasy and deviation, corruption and erosion, a minority remains steadfast and lives in the hope of vindication.

They are godly but they do not seem free. They bear burdens and grunt and sweat under a weary life; they are sheep without a shepherd.

Then Jesus comes.

Chapter 6

Jesus
and
My
Humanity

The coming of Jesus is surrounded by mystery. Three of the Gospels (Matthew, Luke, and John) tell different stories about his coming or different versions of the same story. The Gospel of Mark, Acts, and the Epistles of the New Testament are strangely silent about it. But in spite of variations and gaps in the testimony, some common truths about Jesus emerge:

1. Jesus is special. He was sent by God, he was God's son, he was God with us, he was God in human flesh.

2. Jesus came to save us from our sin.

3. In order to save us Jesus had to be like us. So he became like man and appeared in human likeness (Phil. 2:7).

4. In order to save us Jesus had to die and he died the death of a common criminal. But because he thus died in obedience to the mandate of the divine love, God raised him up.

5. Because Jesus was raised from the dead, we may share in his resurrected life.

I believe that there are two ways in which the coming of Jesus may be interpreted. The conventional way is to see in Jesus the divine Savior who helps us to be better people. We are bad but Jesus can make us good. He can do this by being an example of goodness and by making a power available to us which has been outside our grasp. One of the old gospel hymns says it:

> He died that we might be forgiven,
> He died to make us good.[1]

But the strange thing is that the Jesus who emerges in the Gospels is not this kind of person. His treatment of people suggests that he did not come to make them good. He seems not to have been too fond of good people. He did not even present himself as good. His word to the rich young ruler is significant, "Why do you call me good? No one is good but God alone" (Luke 18:19, RSV).

The second way in which the coming of Jesus may be interpreted is to see it as an act of enablement and blessing. Jesus comes to save us from our sin, and our sin is the distortion of our humanity. We can distort our humanity in two ways. We can think of ourselves as superhuman or as subhuman. If we think of ourselves as superhuman, we try in every way to be morally superior to other people and to control them. If we think of ourselves as subhuman, we try in every way to be as bad as we think we are.

On Being Superhuman

Jesus' major conflicts seem to have been with the first class. He was so entirely himself that he was comfortable with people who were under the censure of the religious ruling class. He ate with tax collectors and with prostitutes; he allowed people of questionable virtue to minister to him. Such behavior had a double effect on the religious Establishment. First, it scandalized them that a teacher in Israel should allow himself to be dirtied by contact with the scum of society. A man, they reasoned, is known by the company he keeps. Secondly, it annoyed them that Jesus seemed to prefer the company of the outcasts to theirs. Jesus met the criticism of the Establishment not by changing his strategy but by interpreting it. He said with loving irony that he had come to heal the sick and not the healthy. Since by their confession they were healthy, would it not be a waste to spend his time with them?

It is my conviction that Jesus was finally betrayed by the religious Establishment not simply because he claimed to be God but because he insisted that God had appeared in the form of a street preacher who dared to identify himself with the whole range of humanity. He was betrayed because he was so nakedly human and so vulnerable that he provided no defense for the Establishment.

Let us suppose that Jesus had said to the common people, "Dear friends, I understand that you have certain criticisms of your leaders. You have told me that they seem self-righteous and censorious; they ask for your money without providing the benefits you would like; now and then they appear indifferent to your hunger, your anxiety, your grief. But let me tell you that they are truly God's servants. Believe me, I have it on the best evidence that if it were not for these priests and teachers and administrators, you would be in a very sorry mess. It is natural for us to resent people in authority, and many of us feel that if we could change places with them, things would really hum. But that is a childish attitude. Instead, we ought to pray for our leaders, obey them cheerfully, pay our temple taxes promptly, and stop criticizing those whom God has placed over us."

If Jesus had said that, I am confident that he would have been allowed the freedom to say almost anything he wanted to say. He could have told his parables and performed a few miracles. He would even have been allowed a few tongue-in-cheek comments about the Jerusalem clique.

But he chose not to be identified with the religious power block—the superhuman crowd. Instead of that he identified with the ordinary people. And I think he did this not because the ordinary people were better but because they knew they were ordinary. They understood that they were sinners and would never be good enough to ascend the hill of the Lord and stand in his holy place. They may have tried, but they knew they would not make it.

On Being Subhuman

But among the dispossessed Jesus had another sort of problem. For there is a sin among the lowly which is less nauseating than arrogance but just as stubborn. That is the sin of subhumanity. I am not sure of the names of the devils Jesus drove out of Mary Magdalene, but one of them must have been self-hatred. For if the testimony of counselors and psychiatrists and pastors is valid, many more people suffer from a low self-estimate than a high one. Somewhere along the toilsome road from babyhood to maturity, they are put down; they ask for bread and are given a stone. Girls asking to be guided through the difficult business of loving a man are turned off by insecure fathers who find it easier to be disciplinarians than persons—or who cannot handle the responsibility of fatherhood and just walk away. Boys struggling toward manhood are caught in the sticky love of their mothers or run head on into fathers who cannot like them. Such rejection is turned inward. The reasoning runs: If I am not loved, I must not be lovable. And if I am not lovable, what good am I?

Alcoholics, drug addicts, prostitutes, and many others of society's miserables are the victims of this basic put-down. For them to be human is to be nothing, and their behavior bears out their estimate of themselves.

Jesus' way of dealing with these people is to affirm them. He encourages the slightest bending of the soul toward healing. He builds on the shakiest foundation. "He will not break off a bent reed,/Nor will he put out a flickering lamp" (Matt. 12:20, TEV).

He affirms the sick by healing them and the captive by making them free, everywhere reinforcing his word that he has come not to be served but to serve and to give his life to redeem many people. His beautiful words recorded by Matthew the evangelist seem designed to deal with the truly despairing person:

> "Come to me, all of you who are tired from carrying your heavy loads, and I will give you rest. Take my yoke and put it on you, and learn from me, for I am gentle and humble in spirit; and you will find rest. The yoke I will give you is easy, and the load I will put on you is light" (Matt. 11:28–30, TEV).

It is unsafe to generalize, but it seems to me that Jesus never shows hostility toward a person who comes to him in genuine need. He is rough on the religious leaders who try to snare him, and in his parables he is merciless toward the merciless. But toward the sinner who will not lift up his eyes he is unfailingly compassionate and affirming.

But a characteristic of Jesus which is not so frequently noted is his willingness to be ministered to. He says that he has not come to be served, and he certainly neither expects nor demands to be cared for. But toward those who serve him he is lovingly grateful. He takes what they offer no matter how it is packaged. There are many instances, but a particularly moving one is that of the woman in the house of Simon the Pharisee.

The woman is a prostitute and must be burdened by the grubbiness and guilt of her profession, for she comes to Jesus under very trying circumstances. He is at dinner with a member of the Establishment—the prominent businessman who is also the teacher of the adult Bible class, if I may use an inexact parallel—and the woman must make her way through a crowd of men toward the only man who seems to understand what she is and how she feels. She places herself at Jesus' feet. She washes his feet with her tears and wipes them with her hair. She kisses them and pours perfume over them.

The reactions of Jesus are significant. She brings the only gift she has—a skill developed in dealing with her numerous lovers—but despite the erotic overtones in the way she handles his body, he lets her be. He lets her give him a gift. That the gift is unusual is clear from the critical comment of Simon, " 'If this man really were a prophet, he would know who this woman is who is touching him; he would know what kind of sinful life she leads!' " (Luke 7:39, TEV). But in accepting the gift, Jesus affirms her and cuts through her despair. He loves her, forgives her, and sends her away in peace, which suggests that we affirm people most effectively by letting them feel that we need them.

What Jesus is saying in all this is that it is O.K. to be human. We need not repudiate our humanity by trying to be better than other men, or reject it by trying to be worse. It's O.K. to be human if we will admit what we are and accept his accept-ance of us. "If we live in the light—just as he is in the light—then we have fellowship with one another, and the blood of Jesus, his Son, makes us clean from every sin. If we say that we have no sin, we deceive ourselves and there is no truth in us. But if we confess our sins to God, . . . he will forgive us our sins" (1 John 1:7-9, TEV).

At a clergy conference some time ago, several ministers shared with me some of their hang-ups in the area of sex and marriage. Clergymen have a special problem with sex, because at a deep level the church expects its ministers to be sexless. The minister is allowed to have problems paying his bills or an-swering his mail; he can deliver mediocre sermons and even get angry now and then. But in his relation to the opposite sex he is supposed to be a Galahad both in his actions and his feelings. We remember Tennyson's description, "My strength is as the strength of ten,/Because my heart is pure."

Well, these ministers were in the process of discovering their humanity. They found themselves powerfully attracted to women in their congregations, and just the attraction, though not acted on, was a problem. I think they came to me because I was supposed to be an aging Galahad who had brought home the Grail with his innocence intact. They believed that if they could open their hearts to me, I could suggest a formula which would give them something special, an armor against the darts of the devil.

This kind of assumption always embarrasses me, although I confess it would help if I could play the part of the innocent. I recall a young officer with whom I served in World War II. He had his own moral freedoms, but he expected me to be a saint. I suppose he counted on my goodness to make up for his lapses. I once shocked and angered him by referring in an offhand way to a normal physical process. He thought such language gross and unbecoming a chaplain.

I am not above the fantasy that I am a holy man. I can see myself cradling my chin in my hand and looking at my brother with priestly wisdom and love, assuming the patronizing attitude which the morally pure sometimes use toward the morally impure. But, of course, it won't do. I have my own hang-ups, and the only armor I can give anybody is openness about what I am. The only armor is the confession that I am human and that I sin, again and again. Because of Jesus I can make that confession. Because of him and his acceptance of me, I can tell it like it is, or at least begin to do so. Even if people don't believe me and won't believe me because they need to have me superhuman, I have still got to say it. I have got to say it because that's what it is to live in the light and to have fellowship and be cleansed.

Jesus' final vulnerability—his suffering, death, burial, and descent into Hades—is also his final affirmation of our humanity. He will go anywhere because of his love for us—even to death and hell. "It was while we were still sinners that Christ died for us," writes Paul (Rom. 5:8, TEV). "The first Adam was made of the dust of the earth; the second Adam came from heaven" (1 Cor. 15:47, TEV). And he came from heaven to enable us to be truly human by living in the light as he indeed lives in it.

Chapter 7

The Holy Spirit and My Relationships

The new thing which emerges in the death and resurrection of Jesus and in the coming of the Spirit is the new family, what the Apostles' Creed calls "The holy Catholic Church, The Communion of Saints." * The new family is a people in whom no one is chosen or blessed in a special way because all are chosen and blessed. And all are now chosen because the chosen one has been rejected. "The . . . stone which the builders rejected has become the head of the corner" (1 Pet. 2:7, RSV).

At the heart of this new community is the cursing of the beloved son, for "cursed is everyone who is hanged upon a tree" (Gal. 3:13, NEB).

* In church usage the term "communion of saints" means both the church militant and the church triumphant. Throughout I use the term in a this-worldly sense for the body of Christ, but nothing precludes its extension to those who constitute the cloud of witnesses. They also inhabit the now.

At the heart of the community is the cross of Jesus:

But now, in union with Christ Jesus, you who used to be far
away have been brought near by the death of Christ. For Christ
himself has brought us peace, by making the Jews and Gentiles
one people. With his own body he broke down the wall that
separated them and kept them enemies. . . . By his death on the
cross Christ destroyed the hatred; by means of the cross he united
both races into one single body and brought them back to God.
So Christ came and preached the Good News of peace to all—to
you Gentiles, who were far away from God, and to the Jews, who
were near him. It is through Christ that all of us, Jews and Gentiles, are able to come in the one Spirit into the presence of the
Father (Eph. 2:13–18, TEV).

Here also is the Holy Spirit, for "by one spirit we were all
baptized into one body" (1 Cor. 12:13, RSV).

It's O.K. to be me and to be human; it's O.K. to be related
and to belong and not to go it alone. The Holy Spirit makes
possible and in a sense commands all three conditions: identity,
humanity, relationship.

The first Pentecost was the birthday of the church, and on
that day a new family was created out of strangely separate
people. Most of them were probably Jewish proselytes of dif-
fering ethnic backgrounds, but after the conversion of Saul of
Tarsus, the whole Gentile world was invited to come into the
new family through faith and baptism. Paul describes how
way-out the Christians must have seemed to their contemporaries:

We are like men condemned to death in the arena, a spectacle
to the whole universe—angels as well as men. We are fools for
Christ's sake. . . . We are weak. . . . We are in disgrace. . . .
To this day we go hungry and thirsty and in rags; we are roughly
handled, we wander from place to place; we wear ourselves out
working with our hands. . . . We are treated as the scum of the

earth, the dregs of humanity, to this very day (1 Cor. 4:9-13, *passim*, NEB).

The amazing thing is that people like these were able to accept themselves as the family of blessing. People without an identity were given a new identity and believed themselves to be the chosen unchosen. "But you are . . . God's own people, that you may declare the wonderful deeds of him who called you out of darkness into his marvelous light. Once you were no people but now you are God's people" (1 Pet. 2:9-10, RSV). There is hardly an epistle in the New Testament, at least there is none from the earlier volcanic years, which does not ring the changes on what it means to be this new house of blessing. We can almost choose at random. Christians call themselves and are called "a chosen race" (1 Pet. 2:9, RSV); "the brethren" (1 Thess. 4:9, RSV); "Abraham's offspring" (Gal. 3:26-29, RSV); "God's chosen" (1 Cor. 1:25-28, RSV); God's "sons and daughters" (2 Cor. 6:18); "God's beloved" (Rom. 1:7, RSV); "God's people" (Phil. 1:1, TEV); "God's people who live in Ephesus" (Eph. 1:1, TEV); "faithful brothers in Christ" (Col. 1:2, TEV).

What this seems to mean is that through the Holy Spirit, people were able to lead two lives: the life in history with all its cultural, social, economic, and even religious differences, and the life in Jesus or in the Spirit, which made brothers and sisters out of Palestinian Jews and proselytes and Gentiles from around the world.

What, we ask, is the nature of this new relationship in Jesus? We say "new" for obviously all life in community involves relationships of some sort. It is, in fact, virtually impossible to be human without relationships. Without other people the individual, if he survived at all, would not be able to speak, think, or feel as a human being.

Human relationships are nevertheless so demanding and

scary, that long before we know what we are doing, we determine to control them by doing what the occasion demands. Very early the child learns what mask to wear and what button to press; he discovers when to speak and when to be silent. He perceives his own strengths and the weaknesses of his adversary and he learns to live in his competence and not to give battle when the outcome is uncertain. Although deep inside he probably wants love more than anything else, he looks at life clearly enough to know that respect is a more salable commodity. Hence he becomes an achiever and draws his ego support and emotional sustenance from all the rewards which society provides for those who play the game.

It is as an achiever of some sort that the ordinary individual establishes and maintains his relationships.* In American society with its emphasis on money as a measure of achievement, many parents relate to their children almost solely in terms of financial control or "things" control. They reward their children by giving them things or money and punish them by withholding the same things. But the achievement relationship is not limited to the moneyed segment of society. In professional or academic circles the medium of exchange is demonstrated expertise of some sort; intellectuality or presumed intellectuality can be just as much an instrument of control as money.† I have shared in enough artistic-philosophical discussions to know that invulnerability is the name of the game. Here as elsewhere you dare not be embarrassed too many times

---

* I recently met a man who described his childhood as a prison in which he survived by being, in his own words, "a good prisoner."

† The "publish or perish" philosophy of many universities and prestigious colleges quantifies intellectual work and seems no less venal than the doctrine of profits and assets which guides the commercial world.

without putting your career in jeopardy and hazarding your place in the community of the elite.

The same holds for piety. Religious parents, by effectively manipulating the anxiety and guilt of their children, can drive them into conformity. In that kind of situation the child buys relationships by playing the pious game, however phony he considers it.

It is a gross overstatement to claim that all human relationships are a game of masks, but the family or group in which honesty is the policy is rare. We have been carefully taught to hide our hurts and weaknesses and to keep a façade at all costs.

In this respect the church is like all other communities. Through the long centuries the Jesus society has strayed away from its origins and has learned to lead from strength and not from weakness. That this was not intended is obvious from the New Testament. Paul writes to the Corinthians:

> Now remember what you were, brothers, when God called you. Few of you were wise, or powerful, or of high social status, from the human point of view. God purposely chose what the world considers nonsense in order to put wise men to shame, and what the world considers weak in order to put powerful men to shame. He chose what the world looks down on, and despises, and thinks is nothing, in order to destroy what the world thinks is important. This means that no single person can boast in God's presence (1 Cor. 1:26–29, TEV).

What this seems to say is that in the presence of Jesus we can remove the façade and drop the mask; we no longer need to lead from our competence but can accept the fact that we are simple and foolish, and indeed both hung-up and sinful. Without rejecting our identity of our gifts we can affirm our common humanity. We can "live in the light—just as he is in the light," and so have fellowship with one another.

This evaluation of competence is not intended to downgrade talents or skills. In the Christian perspective intellectual or aesthetic power must be seen as God's gifts to the individual. To deny those gifts—to sit on them—or to seek to immerse them in the communal process is to falsify the uniqueness of both the individual and his gifts. It is characteristic of Jesus that he did not try to create uniformity. His call to the disciples, "Follow me," was not intended to make everyone like him in the sense of duplicating his personhood. He allowed Peter and John and Judas to remain unchangeably themselves. In fact he glorified their uniqueness by recognizing their particular contributions to the brotherhood. Jesus' word to Peter at Caesarea Philippi is highly significant in this context. "You are a rock, Peter, and on this rock I will build my church" (Matt. 16:18, TEV). The meaning of this passage has been unfortunately obscured by Protestant exegetes who wanted to deprive the Roman church of the biblical base of Petrine supremacy. By a tortuous process the "rock" has been made to mean Peter's testimony, not his person.

This is obviously a shaky reading. If we can disabuse our minds of the question of the authority of the church at Rome, and see the passage in its original setting, what emerges is Jesus' affirmation of Peter's uniqueness as a person, and his underlining of Peter's special powers.

So we are allowed to remain ourselves and to retain our powers. These powers, however, are to be seen not as sources of final security but as "gifts." We cannot live in them, we cannot control them, we cannot claim eminence through them. They are like the manna of the wilderness—to be held briefly in trembling hands. Job says it, "The Lord gives and the Lord takes away;/blessed be the name of the Lord" (Job 1:21, NEB).

To deal with one's powers in this way means to affirm one's

humanity and to pitch one's tent on the shaky volcanic ground of every man. It means to relate to other people not through one's powers but through one's brittleness. The powers remain, but in this posture they are no longer possessions to be saved up and protected from thief and moth. They are riches to be shared. The powers remain, but they are no longer swords and spears by which I conquer and dominate others. They are plows and pruning hooks in the service of the community.

It is only lately that evangelical Christians have seen that to be God's person is not to be doctrinally orthodox or merely individualistically converted, but to be a member of God's family and thus to live in relationship. But even though more and more Christians now see that the family of God is central in the faith experience and that Christianity is a corporate, as much as an individual thing, many of us do not live relationally. We accept the relational as an idea but do not transform it or have it transformed into a life style. It is almost as if we did not trust ourselves to belong to one another.

The reason for this is that the church has neglected the doctrine and the practice of corporate life and has conducted its affairs in conformity with the world. It has majored in organizational efficiency and a mass approach. During the Middle Ages the church tried to build a rival monarchy; in the time of the Reformation the churches paralleled and were captives of the national governments; even the voluntaristic bodies which grew out of the great revivals adopted political means to handle their affairs. Life was motivated and controlled by the speaker's rostrum, and the logistics of the church was handled by powerful committees.

The formalizing of spiritual life by overorganization has been complicated by the need to create large congregations.

The size of the membership has been the measuring stick of the church's power and influence. The effect of organization and bigness has been to conceal the needs of the individual members. By observing an outward conformity to the value system of the church—attending services, paying tithes and offerings, and maintaining moral decorum—the Christian man or woman has been able to hide his or her need for forgiveness, consolation, and encouragement. The clinical pastoral program in the church has helped to alleviate the situation somewhat, by encouraging pastors to receive training in counseling and church members to seek help in critical situations, but it is fair to say that such programs, admirable though they are, have not materially affected the general character of church life. In most instances the church still encourages its members to put their best foot forward, to pretend strength, to build respect, and to help the institution present as impressive a façade as possible to the world.

The failure of the organizational church to meet the relational needs of people does not mean that we can dispense with organization. The Jesus family will always need some sort of logistical envelope. Even the disciples who gathered around Jesus had a treasurer. History makes clear that few if any social organisms, however exalted their aims, live long without a structure which recognizes the realities of power. Gilson justifies the institutionalizing of the Franciscans on the grounds that only by becoming an institution could the Order of Little Brothers perpetuate the mystical theology of St. Francis of Assisi.[1]

But urgent as the need for administration and logistics may be, it cannot justify the abandonment of the relational life. Perhaps the best solution is to accept an institutional schizophrenia and to adopt the old Moravian pattern of the *ecclesiola* *in ecclesia,* the little church in the big church. This means the encouragement of smaller groups or teams within the organizational envelope. On the basis of the best wisdom available to us, it would seem that the Jesus family cannot be composed of more people than can be known personally if they are to be entrusted with the load of our humanity. Ten or twelve such people is certainly the maximum, and often sharing will have to be done with only one other or two or four.*

Perhaps this is the place to say a word about how this process may be most effective in the institutional church. In the first place those who participate in groups or teams will have to be accepting of the institutional envelope and will have to resist the tempting notion that because they feel they are the church in some special sense, they can live without the institution. Even if they decide not to split, there is a second temptation they must avoid: suggesting that they are special and have been entrusted with the copyrighted oracles of God. The corollary of this is that they must avoid at all costs pressuring anyone to get with it and become involved in a group. These procedures smell of an expertise inappropriate to anyone who has only his simplicity and folly to sell.

The other side of the coin is that the institutional church, without committing itself to the group thing, might well serve its own interests by some attentive listening and by providing space for the Jesus family to live within its walls. If relational theology is God's thing for the church, the church will benefit from being as nondefensive as possible about it.

In discussing the body of Christ as relational rather than merely institutional, I have an uncomfortable feeling that I may have drifted from the stance of participant to that of critic.

* For more on this subject, see the Appendix, pp. 171–76.

I have not been confessing a faith or witnessing to an experience so much as analyzing a sociological or religious fact.

But when I talk about the church as relational, I am not speaking from the podium of a church historian but from the warm, pulsating interior of the thing itself. I am a confessor of the relational church.

From time to time I shall no doubt slip into the professional mode. (Now that mode is O.K. in its place and needs no defense from me.) But in this context I do not want to be a professor but a confessor.

Chapter 8

Living
in
the
Light

W̲e have spoken of the Jesus family as a relational possibility within the institutional church. What does it mean to be a member of that family?

It means not some mystical experience in which, like Paul, we are transported to the third heaven, or even a psychic happening crammed with lights and colors, but quite simply presenting ourselves as we are to the family of faith with our whole spectrum of human feelings.*

Some years ago a young woman who was having some trouble admitting feelings told me of an experience she had had as a ten-year-old. Her family had driven to the home of

---

* I obviously do not object to transport and happening. People growing in self-acceptance in the Holy Spirit and finding both vulnerability and affirmation write to me in exactly those terms. They have a foretaste of heaven or feel themselves translated to the "third heaven." Amen! So be it.

her grandparents, of whom she was very fond, and as the car pulled up to the door, she dashed up the steps of the porch shrieking her delight. But her mother pulled her up short, reprimanding her for her unseemly exuberance and telling her that nice girls learn to control their feelings.

No doubt the mother had good motives. To live in the world means that we cannot do what we want to when we want to do it. But good manners easily become a strait jacket for feelings, and we sacrifice good human looseness for a frozen decorum.

To be a Christian in the first century meant to be honestly human—to live in the light. The Epistle of James states it with authentic primitive flavor:

> Is there any one of you who is in trouble? He should pray. Is any happy? He should sing praises. Is there any one of you who is sick? He should call the church elders, who will pray for him and pour oil on him in the name of the Lord. This prayer, made in faith, will save the sick man: the Lord will restore him to health, and the sins he has committed will be forgiven. Therefore, confess your sins to one another and pray for one another, so that you will be healed (James 5:13-16, TEV).

In the Jesus family, James seems to say, health, both spiritual and physical, depends on communicating what is inside of us to God and to one another. We can pray to God directly about our troubles, we can rejoice, we can ask for prayers and for anointing with oil if we are sick, we can confess to one another and pray for one another.

What has happened to this kind of honesty? Because of our Spartan training and our pioneer mentality, or perhaps because of the demands to be civilized, most of us find it difficult to admit we are in trouble, or sick, or guilty. And because of the-Lord-knows-what hang-ups, we do not even dare to express our happiness until we have been fortified with a few drinks. Presumably this is because it is foolish to seem too happy. After all, a variety of miseries may strike us at any moment and turn our joy into sorrow. Hence it is more manageable to stay grim or at least neutral and leave the exuberance to children.

The Posture of Perfection

To live in the light is to admit that we are human and that, in spite of the presence of the Holy Spirit, we remain human. This does not mean that we are to presume on grace and to sin that grace may abound, for sin remains sin. But neither are we to construct a phony facade of piety which is designed to conceal our humanity. "If we say that we have no sin, we deceive ourselves and there is no truth in us."

Throughout the history of the church this has been a hard saying, and many efforts have been made to circumvent it by various doctrines of perfection. Since, it has been argued, Christ has translated us into the kingdom of grace, we ought to be different from other people, more than human. It is not necessary to review all the different forms of this doctrine. It was apparently already popular at the time of the writing of 1 John and it still lives on in some evangelical circles. I have called it "the posture of perfection." It develops from the assumption that grace is sufficient to change human life and behavior radically, and that a person once transformed by it should be able to live his life on a plane of victoriousness unavailable to the unsanctified. The ills that ordinary flesh is heir to—the pains, the griefs, the rages, the lusts, the erosions—should lose their sting and the believer should be able to rise above his humanity into a kind of saintliness.

The posture may be an effort to safeguard the life-giving

moment of conversion and to make it permanent. There are unquestionably times when we manage to transcend ourselves and to feel a calm and a joy which are close to ecstasy. The perfectionist assumes that this can be made a permanent state and sets about to make it such by his own kind of ritual.

He also manages to make other people believe that this is a normal state for Christians and that pushed-under feelings are evidence of a special degree of sanctity. The result is a host of Christian people who dare not have normal feelings or to express them because to do so is to cast aspersions on God's power to keep them. The "cheerful" Christian who dares not show pain or irritation, the joyous Christian who does not grieve, the loving Christian who is never angry, the serene Christian who is never ruffled, the calm Christian who is never anxious or fearful, the clean Christian who is not troubled by his sexuality—all of these in one way or another manifest the posture of perfection.

There is a helpful passage in Augustine's *Confessions* on the handling of human feelings. Soon after the conversion of Augustine in A.D. 387, his mother Monica died. The relationship between the two had been very close. Monica had played a significant role in Augustine's conversion and had helped to steady the first steps of his Christian pilgrimage. Then, suddenly, she was dead. Though overwhelmed with grief, he did not want to spoil his witness to the pagans by what seemed to him an unseemly sorrow; hence he swallowed his feelings. The result was a depression which Augustine analyzes with almost clinical precision.

> But when she breathed her last, the boy Adeodatus [Augustine's son by his concubine] burst out into a loud lament; then, checked by us all, held his peace. In like manner also a childish feeling in me, which was, through my heart's youthful voice, finding its

vent in weeping, was checked and silenced. For we thought it not fitting to solemnize the funeral with tearful lament, and groanings. . . .

. . . But in Thy ears, where none of them heard, I blamed the weakness of my feelings, and refrained my flood of grief, which gave way a little unto me; but again came, as with a tide, yet not so as to burst out into tears, nor to a change of countenance; still I knew what I was keeping down in my heart. And being very much displeased that these human things had such power over me, which in the due order and appointment of our natural condition must needs come to pass, with a new grief I grieved for my grief, and was thus worn by a double sorrow.

And behold, the corpse was carried to the burial; we went and returned without tears. For neither in those prayers which we poured forth unto Thee . . . did I weep . . . ; yet was I the whole day in secret heavily sad, and with troubled mind prayed Thee, as I could, to heal my sorrow, yet Thou didst not. . . . It seemed also good to me to go and bathe, having heard that the bath . . . drives sadness from the mind. . . . I bathed, and was the same as before I bathed. For the bitterness of sorrow could not exude out of my heart. . . .

And then little by little I recovered my former thoughts of Thy handmaid, her holy conversation towards Thee, her holy tenderness and observance towards us, whereof I was suddenly deprived: and I was minded to weep in Thy sight, for her and for myself, in her behalf and in my own. And I gave way to the tears which I before restrained, to overflow as much as they desired; reposing my heart upon them; and it found rest in them, for it was in Thy ears, not in those of man, who would have scornfully interpreted my weeping.[1]

Our own situation may parallel that of the great Latin father. We may be frightened, anxious, sad, greedy, lustful, and half a hundred other things. But we dare not reveal these feelings, for to do so would spoil our image and our witness. We prefer to keep people in the dark about our humanity.

Some years ago I made a public, half-humorous allusion to a mad last-minute dash I had made to get my income tax return to the post office by the midnight deadline. A friend, who seemed more concerned than I was about my image, criticized me for my confession on the grounds that I should be an example of punctuality for the younger generation. I believe that what troubled my friend was not so much my weakness as my public revelation of it. We must at all costs appear to be models of moral strength and manly virtue.

But, to paraphrase John, "If we say we have no feelings and are goof-free, we deceive ourselves and the truth is not in us. But if we confess our humanity, God is faithful and just. . . ."

Honesty and the Fellowship

We are helped to such honesty about ourselves by the fellowship. Not too long ago, an incident occurred which made me very angry. I was so angry that I became incoherent. I literally could not speak. But my silence was ironically interpreted by some of my friends as maturity, control, even gentleness. It was only after one of my colleagues encouraged me to be honest about my feelings, that I understood how badly I had managed them and what rage I was sitting on. I had tried to be a Christian by floating above my anger and had only succeeded in evading the light. It took my friend's candor to lead me back into it.

To live in the light is also to be vulnerable—to live so nondefensively that I allow myself to be wounded. Most children are vulnerable. They walk into things with their defenses down. They do not know how, or they forget, to guard their noses against flying fists. But they learn very soon from their more cynical playmates that unguarded noses get hurt, and they begin to develop the manly art of self-defense.

To be nondefensive is thus a very rare achievement, and it is virtually impossible without a team—a fellowship. In fact, it requires a rare fellowship. Most churches support the defensiveness of their members and are reluctant to accept vulnerability. Let one of the flock begin to express doubts and fears and he is immediately surrounded by well-meaning saints who try to glue him back together again. It is a terrible thing to fall into the hands of saints who have forgotten that they are human. In their frantic need to restore equilibrium and to keep God on the throne, they will resort to evasion, dishonesty, and a series of stereotypes such as "Christ is the answer" or "Prayer changes things" or "Let's get back to the Bible." All of these statements have validity, but used defensively they tend to cut short a necessary process of working things out or through—what might be called creative wrestling.

Process

Among the defensive devices used to keep us invulnerable is a strategy called *guidance*. Now guidance used in the biblical sense is one thing. It implies that God rules in the affairs of men and that I can trust his providence to bring me where I am supposed to go. But providence in the biblical sense does not eliminate process. It works through process. It engages man in the full exercise of his powers; it pushes him to the utmost limits of his human resources; it lets time melt away in a series of false starts or baffling circularities; it may even underscore his physical frailty and impermanence.

Witness, for example, Jacob's wrestling with God at Peniel.

This is a dark story filled with racial memories and half-formed ideas about the goodness of God. It is also a throwback to Jacob's deception of Isaac and his cheating Esau of the blessing. (Now Jacob asks for the blessing directly from the hand of God.) But dark as the story is, it speaks to us at a deep level of what it is to be human and what it is to fall into the hands of the living God. It is guidance through process.

Another example of providence which works through process is the wilderness wandering of the children of Israel. Why, we ask, if the people of God moved at the command of God, was it necessary to have them stumbling around in the desert for forty years. God delivered them quickly from the power of the Egyptians; why did he not immediately give them entrance into Canaan? The answer is found on every page of the Bible. Biblical faith stresses God's mediate actions. He works through people and through the texture of human life, not because his power is limited but because it is in this way he achieves his purpose with us.

The most telling example of process is the Incarnation itself. The Word becomes flesh in a special act of God, but he is born to a human mother in the way all children are born. He grows the way children grow, he lives the way people live. He manifests the power of God, but he does not use any special powers to pole-vault over difficulties. In the night in which he is betrayed, he too wrestles with God and asks that the cup might pass from him.

Biblical guidance thus stresses our humanity and God's activity in it. It is intended not to make us invulnerable but vulnerable. It is designed to stretch us not because God is reluctant to love us but because he loves us so much that he wants us to be people and not puppets.

There is another doctrine of guidance which ignores process. It is derived originally from the Oxford Group movement and proceeds on the assumption that God will lead me in almost any particular act if I am willing to be led. All I need to do is to make my mind a blank page on which God will write his will for me. The way to get guidance is to be quiet before God and to wait for his voice. In effect I suspend my critical judgment, my feelings, and even my intuitional response and wait for a naked revelation from God. Once I get this guidance, I am lifted above the fallibilities with which I normally struggle and am home free.

It is not my intention to put down this doctrine of guidance because it is illogical. Most doctrines of prayer and guidance are illogical, including my own. My reason for rejecting it is that it violates the Christian doctrine of personhood revealed in the Scriptures. It seeks to circumvent my humanity and to give me a foolproof way to arrive at knowledge of God's will.

Having said this, I would like to reiterate that I believe in guidance, in prayer, and in miracle. I believe that God's power is active in human life and that now and then he acts nakedly. There have been occasions when he has been fit to rescue me or my project even when I did not do my homework. But I wouldn't want to presume on that. Most of the time he uses us as servants, and that means that he is pleased to work through our service.

He is also pleased to work through our ordinariness. He accepts us as people who fail and sin and need to be forgiven and restored. The communion of saints needs to keep this truth in focus and to resist the illusion that its achievements are special. Nothing so alienates the church from the world as the pretensions of professional holiness. People may believe in God and find many things in the faith credible, but they can't stomach being patronized by invulnerable people who seem to have solved all their problems.

Holden Caulfield says it in *The Catcher in the Rye:*

> In the first place, I'm sort of an atheist. I like Jesus, and all, but I don't care too much for most of the other stuff in the Bible. Take the Disciples, for instance. They annoy the hell out of me, if you want to know the truth. They were all right after Jesus was dead and all, but while he was alive, they were about as much use to him as a hole in the head.[2]

A vulnerable communion of saints encourages my vulnerability and keeps me from shifting gears and moving from humanity back into that expertise we call saintliness. The Apostle Paul knew such saintliness as Pharisaism. It had once been his primary credential, and the temptation to lean on it seems to have remained with him a long time. In his letter to the Christians in Philippi he speaks of it as "confidence in the flesh." Such confidence is a leading from strength. It means relating to people in terms of my performance rather than my humanity and weakness. And Paul knew it as temptation. In dealing with the new Christians in the various churches, Paul found his authority as an apostle under constant challenge. Who was this physically unpretentious and rhetorically ineffective traveler who claimed the right to guide the churches and even to discipline them?

Paul was undoubtedly tempted to tell them of his past achievements—*You don't know who I am? Well, let me set you straight.* "If anyone thinks he can be safe in external ceremonies, I have even more reason to feel that way. I was circumcised when I was a week old. I am an Israelite by birth, of the tribe of Benjamin, a pure-blooded Hebrew. So far as keeping the Jewish law is concerned, I was a Pharisee, and I was so zealous that I persecuted the church. So far as a man can be righteous by obeying the commands of the Law, I was without fault" (Phil. 3:4–6, TEV).

It was, of course, no way to go. Paul's credential was no longer any special sort of piety or zeal or standing in the Jewish religious community. His credential was a noncredential: identification with the crucified Jesus. This emerges clearly in the sentences which follow:

> But all those things that I might count as profit I now reckon as loss for Christ's sake. Not only those things [i.e., his Pharisaic credentials]; I reckon everything as complete loss for the sake of what is much more valuable, the knowledge of Christ Jesus my Lord. For his sake I have thrown everything away; I consider it all as mere garbage, so that I might gain Christ, and be completely united with him. No longer do I have a righteousness of my own, the kind to be gained by obeying the Law. I now have the righteousness that is given through faith in Christ, the righteousness that comes from God, and is based on faith. All I want is to know Christ and experience the power of his resurrection; to share in his sufferings and become like him in his death, in the hope that I myself will be raised from death to life (Phil. 3:7–11, TEV).

At the heart of Pauline faith is the paradox that his only achievement is a gift. He will not deny his gifts, but he will not see them as permanent possessions, as money in the bank. He will not be a professional saint.

The Professional Church

Despite this refreshing amateurishness in Paul, the church has historically gone professional. It has clung to its track record; it has lived by its specialness. In the Roman church the "religious"—bishops, priests, monks, nuns—have developed vicarious saintliness for the benefit of other people. In Protes tantism ministers and professional missionaries have been seen as exemplars—model Christians. It has been my privilege to know many priests, ministers, and missionaries who reject the role their communities have fashioned for them and who fight to be real people, but they have the institution against them.

I recall being singularly depressed by an ecumenical missionary hostel I once visited. I didn't mind the austerity of the facilities; they had a clean, Spartan air which reminded me of a military camp, and that was O.K. What bothered me was the dampness of the mood. I recalled T. S. Eliot's irreverent line, "the damp souls of housemaids." [3] The effort to play the missionary role was so strenuous that all frivolity and even risking were washed out. People seemed unblessed, dour, filled with suppressed rage. They did not seem to like what they were doing. Even the occasional humor had a guilty air. The total posture seemed based on the need to appear "different" from the world. The sobriety of the clothes, the solemnity of the mien, the muffled, melancholy tones of the voice, the tightly reined feelings conspired to create a sterile image totally alien from the tropical luxuriance which surrounded us and the healthy sensuousness of the people whom the missions were designed to serve.

But while we are seeing the mote in the eye of the institutional church, it is well not to forget the beam in our own. The nonconventional, emerging church has its own temptations, and relational theology can easily become a new kind of invulnerability. I see my relational insights as so precious and so effective in the liberation of up-tight people that I develop my own posture of perfection and my own pontificate. In the conventional church my pretensions may be modified by the very structure I serve. If I am a bishop, I am bound by the traditions and the protocol of bishops. But in the nonconventional church I have no historical models, no fathers, no disciplining traditions. My charisma may have no control at all. I can dream the wildest nonsense, initiate the most destructive iconoclasms, go dressed in a pleated toga or dance naked in the public streets, and if that is my thing, who is to question it? "The state, it is I."

Thus I, who may have laughed at professional holiness, fall into an even more intolerable stance, and my vulnerability glitters with a steely arrogance.

The only antidote I know to such madness is a family of human people who trust the Holy Spirit and who, in the midst of distortion and confusion, affirm their humanity and risk laughing at the idols their own creativity may have fashioned.

To laugh at my pretensions of holiness and infallibility may be the first step toward a confession of my sins. And the communion of saints is the context in which I claim the grace of confession.

In the primitive church there seems to have been a well-established practice of confession. James urges his readers to confess their sins to one another that they may be "healed," and in John's Gospel there is a word of the risen Lord relating the forgiveness of sins by the fellowship to the receiving of the Holy Spirit. The words are as follows: "He said this, and then breathed on them and said, 'Receive the Holy Spirit. If you forgive men's sins, then they are forgiven; if you do not forgive them, they are not forgiven'" (John 20:22–23, TEV).* The words are not unlike those of Jesus to Peter at Caesarea Philippi

---

* It is tempting to see in this postresurrection word of Jesus the kernel of the third article of the Apostles' Creed which associates the Holy Spirit with the communion of saints and the forgiveness of sins.

which Matthew places immediately before the Transfiguration but which some scholars feel have a postresurrection ring, "I will give you the keys of the kingdom of heaven, and whatever you bind on earth shall be bound in heaven, and whatever you loose on earth shall be loosed in heaven" (Matt. 16:19, RSV).

Regardless of the historic situation in which Jesus spoke these words, they were interpreted by the infant church as a mandate to confess sins and to forgive or absolve. It is probable that, to begin with, the entire fellowship heard the particular failures and transgressions of their brothers and sisters and had the opportunity to give them the assurance of forgiveness.

Out of this practice grew the sacrament of penance in the Roman church. Instead of confessing publicly, the penitent shared his guilt only with the priest in what came to be called "auricular" confession, that is, a confession spoken directly into the ear. Even this rite was further depersonalized by the use of the confessional, a box in which the priest sits to hear confession and by which contact is limited to that of the voice.

Auricular confession was valuable in many ways. It was deficient in that it no longer entrusted the task of "binding" and "loosing" to the communion of saints, but devolved the responsibility on a professional person, but it did allow a human agent to play a role in healing.

Even this was lost in the Reformation. The role of the priest in the entire process of penance was questioned, along with the mediatorial role of the church, and confession became a general rite which practically had little, if any, personal meaning. In the eighteenth and nineteenth centuries the folk revivals had the effect of limiting the confessional act to what a man might say to God privately. Such a denial of the validity of confession to other Christians was an understandable effort to correct Roman abuses, but it overshot itself and even denied clear scriptural authority for the confessional grace which is mediated by Christians to Christians.

It is probable that the change from public to auricular confession came about from the unwieldiness of the former in growing congregations. It was not physically impossible for thousands of people to confess publicly to one another; it was psychologically infeasible and led to a number of abuses.

The problem of public confession in our large congregations still exists and argues for the division of our churches into manageable cells, teams, groups, or blocks without the destruction of the institutional envelope. Among evangelicals in South America the block church serves the need of close personal contact, and in America the underground or house church has a similar function. Only in such small groupings can relationships develop and people learn what it means to walk or live in the light, as God is in the light, and have fellowship with one another, in the assurance that "the blood of Jesus . . . makes us clean from every sin."

Chapter 9

The Grace of Affirmation

Being a member of the Jesus family has a further meaning. Just as it is a grace to walk in the light, to confess what we are and to be cleansed and restored to fellowship, so it is also a grace to affirm others. The Incarnation is God's act of total affirmation of beings who have tried in every way to separate themselves from him.

Jesus

To affirm another person is to restore his sense of worth both as an individual and as a human being. Jesus was skillful in affirming people, particularly those who had been put down by the religious community. He looked at people who were despised by the pious—tax collectors and prostitutes and gentiles—not only compassionately but appreciatively. He pitied them, to be sure, but he also honored them. He celebrated the gifts and graces he found in them.

Jesus affirmed people by making them feel that they were worth his time and care. In the Gospels he spends a great deal of time being responsive to their frankly stated needs. They are sick or crippled or have ailing children and servants; they are hungry, tired, anxious, guilty. Most of them want to be helped. They have translated their need into willing and believing. They are importunate. They waylay Jesus, they "press upon him to touch him," they raise their voices in cries for help, they bring their sick, they thrust their children on him, they argue with him, they douse him with expensive perfume, they ask him tough questions, they praise him extravagantly. Sometimes he walks away from them because he is fatigued or overwhelmed. But he never puts them down. He honors their need and their willingness to focus it and express it in an act of faith. Some of his sayings and parables show his appreciation for prayer as the focusing of need in a single importunate act. "Ask, and it will be given you; seek, and you will find; knock, and it will be opened to you" (Matt. 7:7, RSV). To such importunity he is always responsive.

Jesus also affirmed people by assuring them that he needed them. His dependence on his disciples and more particularly on the inner circle—Peter, James, and John—his intimacy with the Bethany family, his gracious acceptance of the ministry of the harlot in the house of Simon, and his visit to the house of Zacchaeus—all these suggest our Lord's need of people and his affirmation of them.

Paul

The Apostle Paul shows the same beautiful sensitivity toward people. In one of his gentlest letters and one of the first we have preserved from his pen, 1 Thessalonians, the tone is consistently affirmative and encouraging. He begins by telling the Christians in Thessalonica that they have been modeling the faith for the believers in Macedonia and Achaia and, in fact, "everywhere where the story of your faith in God has become known" (1:8, Phillips).

He reviews with them how tenderly he dealt with them in the infancy of their faith. "Our attitude among you was one of tenderness, rather like that of a devoted nurse among her babies. Because we loved you, it was a joy to us to give you not only the Gospel of God but our very hearts—so dear did you become to us" (2:7–8, Phillips).

Paul also affirms the faithful by expressing his need of them. After leaving Thessalonica and traveling on to Athens, his need for contact with the Thessalonians became so acute that he sent Timothy back to his friends to strengthen and encourage them. And Timothy brings back a report on which Paul comments:

> Now that Timothy has just come straight from you to us—with a glowing account of your faith and love, and definite news that you cherish happy memories of us and long to see us as much as we to see you—how these things have cheered us in all the miseries and troubles we ourselves are going through (3:6–7, Phillips).

It is quite probable that nothing so affirmed and cheered the Thessalonians as this confession of the Apostle that he needed them. We all need to be needed. To know that people depend on us and that we are important to them heals the wounds of our insecurity and helps us to affirm others.

What It Is Not

We may be helped to understand affirmation by also knowing what it is not.

(1) It is obviously not flattery. Flattery is a tactic designed to manipulate people for evil ends. The serpent in the garden was a flatterer; so were the false prophets in the court of Ahab. In Dante's *Inferno* flatterers are immersed in a lake of liquid dung. To tell people what they want to hear in order to con them into serving me is flattery. It is deceptive affirmation and it has a negative effect. The flattered person feels duped and put upon. Though he may respond momentarily to the pleasing words, he carries a residue of resentment.

(2) It is not mere commendation of obvious strengths. To tell a beautiful woman that she is beautiful, or an outstanding athlete that he plays well may not be affirmation at all. In order to be affirmed, the beautiful woman may need to be told that she has the capacity for friendship or the athlete that he is sensitive to people. Thus, at heart, affirmation is a response to the human cry, to what the person truly is, wishes to be, or intends to become. Browning comes close to the secret in *Rabbi ben Ezra:*

> Not on the vulgar mass
> Called "work" must sentence pass,
> Things done, that took the eye and had the price;
> O'er which, from level stand,
> The low world laid its hand,
> Found straightway to its mind, could value in a trice:
>
> But all, the world's coarse thumb
> And finger failed to plumb,
> So passed in making up the main account;
> All instincts immature,
> All purposes unsure,
> That weighed not as his work, yet swelled the man's amount:
>
> Thoughts hardly to be packed
> Into a narrow act,

Fancies that broke through language and escaped;
All I could never be,
All, men ignored in me,
This I was worth to God, whose wheel the pitcher shaped.

(3) Affirmation is not a social unguent spread over tension and conflict. In a time which is discovering the value of honesty and telling it like it is, which encourages gripe sessions and sensitivity (both of which are, in part, telling people how they "come through" to us), affirmation may sound like Madison Avenue or, worse yet, phoniness. In the 1920s when America was moving into the first stages of defensiveness about its modern image, Sinclair Lewis invented the character of Babbitt who, together with his time, was hypersensitive about criticism. The Babbitts encouraged Americans to throw away their hammers (negativism) and buy a horn (positiveness).

To buy and blow your horn in the 1920s meant to ignore social ills and to avoid rocking the boat. Affirmation may sound like that to some contemporary Americans. But there is an important difference. In the tradition of Jesus, affirmation is directed not toward silencing social criticism, but toward discovering and encouraging the worth of the unaffirmed. The social dimension of affirmation is recognizing the rights of minority peoples and celebrating their worth.

(4) Again, affirmation is not sentimentality. To affirm is not to deny the warping of sin or to assume pure motives. My affirmation will consequently risk an ambiguity. It will suggest that I am condoning that in the other person which is not good. Jesus ran that risk in his dealings with tax collectors and thieves and harlots. For him to go to Zacchaeus's house could have been interpreted as indifference to fraud; to be accepting of the street woman in the house of Simon could have been read as indulgence toward immorality. But he ran

the risk. He did not gloss over evil but neither did he condemn people. He said to the woman taken in adultery, "Nor do I condemn you. You may go; do not sin again" (John 8:11, NEB).

(5) Finally, affirmation is not depriving God of honor. That this is a fear of some people is clear from the often repeated cliché, "And God shall have all the honor." The fear seems to rest on the assumption that God is jealous of us and that he needs to appropriate every crumb of commendation for himself, leaving none at all for his creation.

I grew up in this tradition and was made to feel guilty about praise. In one of the churches I served while still a very young man, it was a tradition to honor the members on every conceivable occasion. Birthdays, anniversaries, the recovery from illness, the return from a trip—all became opportunities for celebration. I was aware that my little congregation was made up of first-generation immigrants and their children and that for them the church was the only meaningful context in American society—an island in a sea of troubles. Hence for psychological reasons, if for no other, they needed the affirmation they would not be getting from the larger community.

But I had a residue of moralism in myself and the beginnings of some theological sophistication, and I found this endless thanking and praising of people spiritually inappropriate. It was my understanding that God and not people should be honored, although, with beautiful inconsistency, I was not averse to the adulation I sometimes sopped up after my sermons on Sunday morning.

One of the leaders of the church, a straightforward, practical man with a streak of unbelievable stubbornness in him which made him insensitive to my theological refinements, used to justify the various parties held by reading from Romans 12:10, which, in the Swedish translation, is very close to the Revised

Standard Version: "love one another with brotherly affection; outdo one another in showing honor." For him "showing honor," unlike the mousy King James Version "in honor preferring one another," meant affirmation of people: parties with lots of cakes and, since we were not in the ale tradition, strong coffee. It has taken me a long time to understand how right he was.

Discerning Gifts

Affirmation, at a deeper level, means also the discernment of gifts.* The question of "gifts" in the New Testament sense is complicated and needs more serious consideration than I can give it in these brief pages. But a few things are clear.

In the first place the New Testament gifts alluded to in 1 Corinthians 12–14 are not what we usually call talents. Talents are natural capacities which I can discern rather readily in myself. The talent to sing—or to draw, to think, to write, to excel in sports, or to lead—is usually something which emerges fairly early in my life and I can devote myself to its cultivation or not as I choose.

Talent belongs to the order of creation; its use or nonuse is important in the establishment of our identity and in our life in the human family, but it has too often been confused with the gifts and graces which belong to the order of salvation. Thus a bright, articulate boy growing up in a pious family is sometimes made to feel that his talent belongs to the church and that he ought to become a minister. Young people less talented are made to feel that the bright, articulate boy is more "gifted" and hence of greater value to the kingdom.

* See a helpful discussion of gifts in Bruce Larson and Ralph Osborne, *The Emerging Church* (Waco, Texas: Word Books, 1970), pp. 57–59.

Thus there grows up a de facto barrier between clergy (the talented) and the laity (the untalented).

Gifts are not talents, although they need not be mutually exclusive. The gifts of apostleship, teaching, and prophecy, for example, cannot be independent of certain intellectual powers, but the powers themselves do not constitute the gift. Perhaps talents and powers must be crucified and raised again before they can function as gifts.

In the passage in 1 Corinthians 12–14 we have alluded to, it is clear that the members of the church do not bring their gifts to the church; the gifts are distributed to the believers by the Holy Spirit after the church has come into existence, on the basis of what is needful for the body of Christ. The exercising of the gift is primarily for the good of the whole body and only secondarily for the edification of the individual.

If this distinction between talents and gifts is valid, then it is evident that the organized church has frequently ignored its gifts. It has been so eager to discover the musical, or organizational, or intellectual talents of its members that it has failed to see that the inner life of the church is dependent on something different: the endowments of the Holy Spirit.

Three questions suggest themselves to us at this point: What are the gifts of the Spirit? How are they discerned? How are they to be used in the strategy of the church?

(1) *What are the gifts of the Spirit?* Again, we cannot devote ourselves to an exhaustive study of the question of gifts as it emerges in the New Testament but must limit ourselves to some well-known passages from the pen of the Apostle Paul. The first of these is Romans 12, the second 1 Corinthians 12–14, the third Ephesians 4.* Paul is not a systematic theo-

---

* The list in Ephesians 4:11 includes only five gifts: apostleship, prophecy, evangelism, feeding (the work of the pastor), and teaching.

logian and his categories are never exhaustive. They are rather "for instance" categories, and we are left with the intriguing riddle of whether Paul would have said more or said it differently if the occasion had been different. Be that as it may, let us arrange the lists of gifts in Romans and 1 Corinthians side by side to determine similarities. I have used the descriptions in several versions to try to achieve clarity.

Romans 12	1 Corinthians 12:8–11	12:27–30
preaching	speaking with wisdom	apostles
serving others	speaking with knowledge	prophets
teaching	faith	teachers
stimulating faith (Phillips)	healing	workers of miracles
giving	working miracles or great deeds (Phillips)	healers
wielding authority (Phillips)	prophecy	helpers
feeling sympathy (Phillips)	distinguishing spirits	administrators
	tongues	speakers in tongues
	interpreting tongues	interpreting tongues

It is clear that there are similarities in the lists. We can, for example, identify "teachers" with "speaking with knowledge" and "wielding authority" with "administrators." Healing occurs in two of the lists, and serving and helping are probably similar. But what is more evident is the looseness of the designations. The Apostle seems to have no interest in crossreference and no real concern for finding in Rome what he had encountered in Corinth. If this is the case, we are justified in concluding that the gifts of the Spirit will vary from time to time and from place to place and that there is nothing unbiblical about identifying a range of spiritual gifts in our contemporary churches to which Paul never even refers.

The question "What are the gifts of the Spirit?" must hence be answered in a very tenuous fashion. There are criteria, of course. They must originate in the Holy Spirit, and they must edify the body of Christ. This means that there is a biblical base line. The church is not a cult which has the luxury of developing its own acts. But within biblical bounds, gifts can have an ad hoc character. They can and should be addressed to particular, concrete needs in the life of the fellowship and the community it serves.

(2) *How are the gifts discerned?* Another difference between talents and gifts is that I can discern my talent but not my gift. If the gift is a power or a capacity given to a member of the church by the Holy Spirit for a specific situation, it follows that the Spirit and the church in concert discern what it is and how it is to be used. The gift of prophecy (which I understand to be a revelation given to someone in a particular situation and applicable to it) must surely be discerned and applied by the church if it is to serve the whole body and not merely indulge an individual believer's need for the dramatic. The same applies to healing, evangelism, administration, serving, and even the curious gift of "feeling sympathy" to which Paul alludes in the Romans passage.

(3) *How are the gifts to be used in the strategy of the church?* Many years ago Reinhold Niebuhr charged the Protestant church with devoting most of its energies to the task of recruitment. He left the impression that the church is so busy filling its ranks that it never gets on with doing battle.

There is certainly validity in the criticism that the institutional church spends an enormous amount of energy in keeping itself going and that many of its outreach programs are determined not so much by the needs of the world as by the internal wants of the church itself. One asks, for example, how many missionary programs have been initiated by pressures from the unevangelized world and how many have been responses to the posture of competing denominations or simply the need to be busy with something which has such wide acceptance. Missions has been for many decades "the thing to do." *

An effective church strategy begins, it seems to me, with the simple but difficult act of hearing the human cry. What are people saying to us about their real needs? Our civilization is skillful in making people feel needs which are at best secondary. The bombardment of TV commercials is directed toward making me feel the need to look better, smell better, sleep better, eat better, feel better, do better. But most of these needs are phony and are only stimulated to make me buy more and more things I do not need or need only superficially. In some ways the church has been involved in the same business. It has ministered to a lot of secondary needs. I am not sure, for example, that attending Sunday morning worship in the average church is a primary human need, or that family prayer is the most important thing in keeping a family together, or that getting everybody to read the Bible is going to make the country significantly moral, or that having people join a church is in itself an objective of major consequence. All of these things have value, of course, but are they responses to the deepest human needs?

* Elisabeth Elliot's novel *No Graven Image* (New York: Harper & Row, 1966) deals perceptively with the question of motivation in mission.

What is the *primal scream* (to use a phrase made popular in recent psychological literature)?[1] Certainly one scream is for relationships. Jesus had compassion on the multitudes because they were as sheep without a shepherd. It is a truism that the Palestinian shepherd has an almost personal relationship to his sheep. To be a sheep without a shepherd was to be lost, unfed, unwatered, unprotected, uncared-for. I am not competent to judge the psychology of sheep and certainly not their metaphysics, but if I understand Jesus, he is saying that for a sheep to be unshepherded was, in effect, to be no sheep at all. Similarly, for a person to be without relationships is to be an unperson.

If this is true, the needs to which the church will address itself are primarily relational, and the program which it devises to meet these needs will also be relational.

The four relationships which have first significance for most of us are to God, to ourselves, to significant others, and to the world. Perhaps a fifth should be added: our relationship to nature.

If these relational needs are to be met, the church, as the body of Christ, must form its strategy in such a way as to meet them. It will have to discern the gifts that the Holy Spirit has given to the various members and devise a program which accommodates itself both to the gifts of the members and to the particular needs the church feels called upon to meet.

Gifts and Needs

This two-pronged (gifts and needs) approach is essential, and the church has often erred by studying neither. It has assumed needs which did not exist or were not very urgent (for example, the need to have aesthetically pleasing sanctuaries and hermetically sealed-off Sunday school rooms for every class and expensively edited and printed educational materials). And it has assumed gifts which did not exist. I know of several evangelical churches which have assumed that everyone has the gift of evangelism. I am not going to challenge the need for evangelism; I will simply assume that the aim of evangelism is to bring people into effective relationships. I want to challenge the notion abroad in some high-powered congregations that everyone is equally endowed with the gift of evangelizing. Not only is this not true; it is not scriptural.

Another error of the church is to ignore gifts other than evangelism as if they did not exist or did not have the same value. But I suspect that Paul is saying something very important when he talks about the members and the gifts being interdependent. We cannot visualize a living church without an evangelistic witness. This is becoming abundantly clear as the church is being purged and restructured under the influence of the young Jesus people. But neither should we think of the church solely in terms of that gift. If the church is to minister to the needs of the whole man, we will need to discover all the gifts Paul lists in Romans 12, 1 Corinthians 12 and Ephesians 4, plus some fresh ones, and see that the strategy of the church is formed in such a way as to use real gifts to meet real needs.

If some churches have erred in the direction of evangelism, others have erred in the matter of social witness and action. To be an evangelist is a gift, but so is being political. Every Christian should have a social concern, but not every Christian need respond to that concern in the same way. If God has appointed some to be apostles and others to be prophets and teachers, he has also appointed some to be demonstrators and petition-circulators and perhaps *provocateurs,* and others to be something else. Not much is gained in the evangelistic church by having the minister manipulate the guilt of those he thinks should be evangelists, and not much more is gained in the activist church by having the minister preach "woe, woe" sermons to those he feels should join his latest assault on the bastions of injustice.

We must begin our program, it seems to me, with the division of the church into functional small groups. These groups will then concern themselves with two primary questions: What are the needs we see inside and outside the church? How may the gifts of the believers be used to meet those needs in a realistic way?

As we have already indicated, both the discernment of gifts and their application to needs is the responsibility not of the individual but of the church (as small group) in concert with the Holy Spirit. This means that guidance is sought by the group for the individual, and when it is received, the road is clear for action.

This responsibility of the church as small group for the action of the individual is closely related to the process of accountability. The individual is accountable to the group for the use of his gift in ministry. This means that although he is not responsible for gifts he has not been given, he is committed to a ministry of the gift he has.

But having a gift does not mean freedom from error. We are not introducing a new priesthood which stands above criticism. To have a gift means understanding that I am not its source, that in my use of it I am accountable to the church, and that it can be withdrawn. In other words, I have the treasure in an earthen vessel and I remain, despite the preciousness of the endowment, a human being prone to failure.

The use of the gift is thus a constant risking, and I live in trembling dependence on the Spirit and the fellowship. In the exercise of my gift I may develop some habits which superficially look like expertise or competence. I may be tempted to think of my gift as an achievement and in my insecurity claim an authority I do not have. But such professionalism brings its own judgment in sterility and unfruitfulness.

When the gifts of the Spirit are no longer believed in or are confused with natural talents or are no longer under the loving discipline of the fellowship and the Spirit, the church has taken the first step toward being an institution which thinks of itself as self-validating. It no longer lives by grace alone.

It may be that such a step is a historic necessity. It may be that the church has had to become a self-validating institution in order to live in the face of heresy and schism. I am not competent to make a historic judgment about that. I am only prepared to say that we can now discern with some clarity how our particular team would fare without the posture of nondefensive openness I have tried to describe in the preceding pages—in other words, without grace.

Chapter 10

Death
and
Resurrection

In this sort of fellowship, this family, how does gracelessness express itself? What is it to sin? It is not, obviously, just doing something bad. All of us do bad things, have negative feelings, think bad thoughts. By *bad* I mean selfish, destructive, sneaky, small. Of course, it's bad to be bad, but it's worse to pretend that bad is good.

Hence, three sins destroy the fellowship: (1) the claim to adequacy—"I am rich and have need of nothing"; (2) concealment—the refusal to share my failure, my hurt, and my anxiety with the fellowship; (3) the cop-out—unwillingness to accept the responsibility of death and resurrection.

1. The claim to adequacy is much closer to us than we imagine. It lurks not only in the more obvious kind of arrogance but in every assertion of humanity, vulnerability, and openness. I recently read a letter to an author about one of his books in which the writer attacked the author for the latter's

lack of openness and vulnerability. But, paradoxically, the letter itself was a classical example of harshness and invulnerability.

I cannot recall writing a book in which I have had to make so many fresh starts as in this one, and the reason for it is that I have been writing about humanity in a superhuman fashion. I find myself criticizing censorious people in a censorious manner.

2. If I cling to the notion, even very briefly, that I am adequate and can handle my own affairs, I begin the process of concealing my real self from the fellowship. I refuse to confess and to seek forgiveness for my little failures and errors, and the longer I delay being open, the more I have to conceal. Soon I begin to lead two lives or three or four, and thus cut myself off from the healing of the body of Christ. The more I am able to keep hidden, the more contempt I feel for the brotherhood. Contempt may even ripen into hatred. This, I suspect, is in part the story of Judas.

3. Concealment leads to the ultimate Christian cop-out, which is the refusal to die in order to rise again. The doctrine of death and resurrection has had many interpretations in the long life of the church. In Paul's theology it means the death of the old man and the coming to life of the new. It has both a present and future meaning. Because of Christ's death and resurrection, which is a primal fact, men may die to the old and rise to newness of life in their daily experience and also at the end of history when "the trumpet shall sound, and the dead shall be raised incorruptible." In the time of the martyrs, death and resurrection were particularly associated with the death meted out to Christian witnesses. Later, entering a monastic order was seen as a kind of Christian dying.

With the coming of the Reformation the New Testament

texts on death and dying were reinterpreted to mean pretty largely Christ's typal death and the believer's identification with it through faith. Martyr deaths and the protracted dying in the religious orders were deprived of their earlier significance.

During the Protestant centuries and probably under the influence of the Pietists, death came to mean the denial of the self not through monastic disciplines or ascetic practices but through humility. The sentiment is clearly stated in John Bunyan's little song: [1]

> He that is down needs fear no fall,
>   He that is low no pride;
> He that is humble ever shall
>   Have God to be his guide.
>
> I am content with what I have,
>   Little be it or much:
> And, Lord, contentment still I crave,
>   Because thou savest such.
>
> Fullness to such a burden is
>   That go on pilgrimage:
> Here little, and hereafter bliss,
>   Is best from age to age.

Closely associated with humility is the notion of poverty and lowliness. Poverty is not a requirement, as in the religious orders of the Roman church, but it does seem to be a desirable condition for the Christian pilgrim. Thus humility gets linked with other-worldliness, and piety comes to mean keeping a low silhouette and living as wormily as possible in this life.

> Here little and hereafter bliss
> Is best from age to age. [2]

In this study, death and resurrection has a meaning different from that of the Roman and most of the Protestant churches. To die does not mean to be a martyr, or monk, or nonconformist pilgrim in the manner of Bunyan. It means quite simply being open to the fellowship. It means to confess one's humanity—needs, problems, feelings, sins—and to accept the encouragement, comfort, and urgings of the church.

Such dying will not approach the horror of violent death or the maceration of the religious life; it may even lack the drama of spectacular humiliation. I am thinking of the long procession of missionaries who have sacrificed their dignity and often the good pride of their children to propagate the gospel in foreign parts, or of ministers who have lived and died thinly in the gross shadows of their parishioners. Honestly exposing one's humanity to one's colleagues has none of this pallor or beauty.

And yet it is a dying—an unclothing. It is to be banally myself and strip away every kind of happy clout in which I go dressed: my wit, my insight, my facetiousness. It is to smell with an interior olfactory nerve every one of my spiritual malodors unfilmed by perfume, and to admit to them. To change the metaphor, it is struggling like a netted fish in the meshes of my excuses, evasions, rationalizations, and finally being still in the presence of grave, and loving, eyes.

To say with sincerity, "I failed, I goofed, I blew it, I confess, I am sorry, forgive me, I am no better than my fathers," may seem, in contrast to the tribulations of Thomas More and St. Perpetua, to be greengrocer sufferings, but underneath the skin there is the same sick reluctance. I am pulled screaming and kicking into the presence of truth.

It would be unendurable if the Spirit and the fellowship did not help me die. The saints encourage and comfort and urge me on, not by the waggling of their fingers but by modeling their own mortality. There is a chorus of voices from the deep spaces, "Lord, be merciful to me, a schnook."

It is debatable if the death or the resurrection is more painful. Paul claims that he doesn't want to be unclothed but clothed upon. But to be pulled out of the water (or the grave) by loving hands, to be clothed in my new humanity, and to remain dependent on these hands for my salvation in the sense that God chooses such instruments to keep me honest—this is a sort of purgation and far from easy.

It is no easier to die in the act of confronting a brother who needs what little candor I have. Much contemporary feedback ("This is the way you are coming through to me," etc.) is a sort of game in which I do not feel especially responsible for what I share. I let the victim of my openness spin off into whatever vortex of self-hatred he has fashioned for himself. That, as we say, is his problem.

But in the *corpus Christi* I do not confront my brother to save my feelings or even to glue the fellowship together. I die for him and with him in the truth because I love him and because there is really no blessedness for me and no joy in heaven so long as he stumbles around like a blind sheep. What makes all this so terrifying is that I know that I am also a blind sheep, and need him to see for me. Yet I must continue to bleat my nonsense.

This is the plight of Paul in his second letter to the church at Corinth. We think of the purple passages, but the letter boils like a pot with a rattling lid. Paul is at once chief of sinners and apostle and schoolmaster and big daddy and martyr and braggart. Every moment he finds himself saying too much or too little; he stresses his right to speak as an apostle and he affirms his weakness—thorns in the flesh and buffeting demons and tears and despair of life and triumphal chariots thundering on to glory. Really a wild scene.

Now, of course, it's possible to have Paul come out smelling like a rose. Most exegetes and expositors do this. They make it seem as if Paul is possessed of a special wisdom which helps him deal with the woolliness of the churches in a successful fashion. The impression is left that Paul knew unerringly when to be tough and when to be tender and that he managed to correct and reprove the church in an exemplary way. I am not at all sure that this was so. What seems to emerge, rather, is a man who at one and the same time needs to stress his authority (his apostleship) and his humanity. Now if you are only an apostle—signed, sealed, and delivered—you can confront your straying sheep with a ponderous authority. You can stroke your chin, beetle your aging brows, and pontificate somberly on the failings of the flock. The discipline may be embarrassing to you or tedious or even painful. But, man, it's not dying!

But to be both an apostle and a human being, that is, a man who needs to wash his feet and relieve his bowels and eat and drink and sleep, that is something else. To be an apostle who dares not forget his humanity and to have to exhort and correct other human beings in the midst of their humanity, that is to die and be buried.

To confront my brother when he needs to be confronted is a bitter death. And the dying is not in the risk of being proved wrong or in the risk of hurting him or in the risk of his temporary anger, but in the risk of rejection. I refuse to share what I ought to share with my brother because I want his approval and his love. If I tell the truth, he may walk away and others may walk away with him. If I level with him, I may be left without a friend. And so I say nothing. I smile and smile and smile and prove a villain.

I want to emphasize at this point that I am not advocating any cheap or hasty sensitivity. There is a sense in which I have got to earn the right to be honest, the right to die. Much of the stuff one reads on sensitivity assumes no prior community. People get together on Saturday afternoon, look at one another, single out people they do not like, and boom! let them have it right between the eyes. I have no doubt that there are people who benefit from this kind of spilling, but it is not what I am talking about. Christian sensitivity assumes the body, the *communio sancti*. It assumes that every act of candor is motivated by unconditioned love. It sees confrontation as an act of death and resurrection both for him who corrects and reproves and for him who is corrected and reproved.

This is the mood of 2 Corinthians 7. Paul has had to write an earlier letter in which he leveled with the Corinthians, a very painful process for him and certainly for them. We pick up the heartbeat.

> For even if that letter of mine made you sad, I am not sorry I wrote it. I could have been sorry about it when I saw that the letter made you sad for a while. But now I am happy—not because I made you sad, but because your sadness made you change your ways. That sadness was used by God, and so we caused you no harm (2 Cor. 7:8-9, TEV).

Christian sensitivity also assumes postoperative care. The corrected person and the correcting one are both taken up in the body; they are not cut adrift to fend for themselves.

The death in this—the risk of rejection—can be accepted in the Christian communion because of the presence of the Holy Spirit. No matter how bitter the dying, the Holy Spirit testifies to the reality of the resurrection.

This is the probable meaning of the bringing together in the third article of the Apostles' Creed of the Holy Spirit, the church, the *communio sancti* ("the church militant and triumphant"), the forgiveness of sin, the resurrection of the body, and the life everlasting.

In the context of openness, confession, correction, forgiveness, restoration, and affirmation, the church may truly celebrate Easter morning. Death has been followed by a rising from the dead. The presupposition is the death and resurrection of our Lord. Because he became a man, we can be human and enter into his vulnerability and his dying. And because God raised him from the dead and we are one with him, we may enter into his resurrection.

Easter morning is God's today—it is the point where what needs to be saved from the past is transformed and given its resurrection body, and it is the point at which what is relevant for the future is integrated into the present. This is where the Jesus people live. Because they have received the blessing in the order of grace and have been accepted into God's new family through the Holy Spirit, they do not need the past either as remorse or nostalgia. They do not need it as remorse because they are freed from guilt. Sin no longer has dominion. They do not need the pain of remorse, the gnawing of conscience (what the medievals called the "again-bite of inwit") to atone for past transgression. And they do not need it as nostalgia—the invoking of a fantasy of past innocence or past beatitude—because the present free and joyous moment, though shot through with frustration and pain, is a better moment than anything embalmed and brought forward from the mausoleum of the past.

To live in God's today also means to be freed from the bondage of anxiety and fantasy for the future. We cannot be freed from either anxiety or fantasy. Both serve their function. But we can be freed from their bondage. The future need not control our present by casting its shadow over it or by giving it a shimmer of unreality.

Let me illustrate. I do not relish the thought of getting old. If Browning's lines from *Rabbi Ben Ezra,*

> Grow old along with me!
> The best is yet to be,

refer to the resurrection and the life which are ours in Jesus, that is one thing. But if they refer to the process of aging itself, I can't accept their validity. I resent what I see age doing to my friends and to me. I do not like the irresistible harvest of death around me. I believe with the New Testament that in some sense death is not natural and normal; rather, it is fruit of a primal horror man perpetrated on himself or had perpetrated on him by the serpent.

But the anxiety I feel in thinking about age or the shimmer I find myself casting over it to save me from its harshness can be dealt with in one of two ways. I can use the anxiety and the fantasy as ways to enrich the present, that is, I can use them medicinally. Or, I can become morbidly fixed in them in such a way as to impoverish the present.

We are saved from this morbid extreme by our life in the fellowship and the presence of the Spirit. We live in God's today. We say with George Allen, coach of the Washington Redskins, when he was criticized for bringing some of his Rams from Los Angeles to Washington, "I am not interested in building for the future. I want a winner today." We can be so busy building for the future, planning for the future, saving for the future, worrying about the future, that we destroy today. The Jesus who was well aware of what his future would be ("Behold, we go up to Jerusalem") said to his disciples, " 'Do not worry about tomorrow; it will have enough worries of its own. There is no need to add to the troubles each day brings'" (Matt. 6:34, TEV).

To be reborn into newness of life by the Holy Spirit day after day is to share *now* in the resurrection of the dead and the life everlasting. It is to be at the party and to drink the wine of the new gladness.

Paul said it to his friends in Corinth:

> For we know that God, who raised the Lord Jesus to life, will also raise us up with Jesus and bring us, together with you, into his presence (2 Cor. 4:14, TEV).

The point is, we shall be together, we are together. Paul and the Corinthians and the rest of us have been, are, shall be in the presence of the Lord Jesus. Wow! It's Easter morning.

> For this reason we never become discouraged. Even though our physical being is gradually decaying [no illusion here], yet our spiritual being is renewed day after day. And this small and temporary trouble we suffer will bring us a tremendous and eternal glory, much greater than the trouble. For we fix our attention, not on things that are seen, but on things that are unseen. What can be seen lasts only for a time; but what cannot be seen lasts forever (2 Cor. 4:16–18, TEV).

WHOOPEE . . . HOSANNA . . . ALLELUIAH . . . CHEERS . . . Wow! . . . *AMEN* . . .

Chapter 11

The Un-party

(a short digression into church history)

The church, as I have known it, has been pretty much the congregation of the unblessed. Perhaps this is why I love it; I harbor so much unblessedness in myself, and the good people who try harder to be better and better are my sisters and brothers.

I understand and empathize with the unfavored sons and daughters who feel that they must make it by being dutiful achievers, saints, martyrs, prayer warriors, Florence Nightingales. I understand also that institutions will be forged from our compulsions to minister to our needs. Unblessed people are inclined to create ascetic machinery: hair shirts, lumpy pads, cold dormitories, flagellation, endless orisons, and a diet of mashed turnips—in other words, the physically painful and repugnant; they will devise moral obstacle courses, marathons, mountain climbs, and vigils to exorcise the demon of guilt and to prove their merit.*

I look backward with a mixture of amusement and sadness to a speech I delivered to my high school graduating class. It was based on Arthur Guiterman's poem, "Hills," in which plains and valleys are scorned for heights. I remember the rhetorical clashing of cymbals with which I intoned the closing lines of the poem:

> God, give me hills to climb
> And strength for climbing! [1]

I love that intense, spiritually sensitive eighteen-year-old and his ideals. I see him set against much in his culture which wanted to flatten him into conformity, to seduce him into acceptance of the mediocre life. I want to shout at him across the misty years, "Keep climbing! Don't knuckle under! Give it to 'em!"

But I also see that too much was demanded of him and that he demanded too much of himself. The bow was bent almost to the breaking point.

The fact is that I am terrified of heights and am never so

---

* One of the saddest chronicles of recent times is Elisabeth Elliot's biography of R. Kenneth Strachan (*Who Shall Ascend?*, New York: Harper & Row, 1968), who was for many years the executive director of the Latin American Mission. The impression one gathers from Mrs. Elliot's well-documented book is that Ken Strachan's missionary labors were not freely assumed but were imposed on him by his devotion to his parents, particularly his mother. Very rarely in reading Strachan's letters, as well as his other utterances, as they are presented by his biographer, are we led to feel that the missionary leader was doing what he wanted to do. He seems never to have gotten to the party but rather to have been all his life a compelled and harried man. His words, "I feel trapped," spoken in the last moments of his struggle against a terminal illness, suggest not only the acute physical suffering in which he found himself but also the way his total ministry may have appeared to him.

uncomfortable as when I have to drive or walk through mountains. I remember with pain and embarrassment a bus trip from Interlocken to Lucerne in the summer of 1966 when I spent much of the time lying on a back seat of the bus in a profuse cold sweat because I did not dare look up into those icy fastnesses or down over the rim of the road into plunging nothingness. In those hours of agony I had more than I needed of Guiterman's hills.

The hills bit is a parable of my existence and of my experience with God. Despite early training in the Lutheran doctrine of grace, and frequent exposure to Paul's writings in the New Testament, I seem to have lived my life as if God expected me to climb Everest. It did not matter that I was unsuited for mountain climbing and feared mountains. Up I had to go. "Who shall ascend into the hill of the Lord?" (Ps. 24:3).

And I have had many fellow pilgrims. A few decades ago the style was evangelical mountain climbing. The faithful arranged wearying schedules of prayer, Bible study, church attendance; they frowned on the pleasure principle and made the body a dreary ass whose only purpose was to drag the soul from one portal of immortality to another; they deplored loveliness and cultivated ugliness; they developed a missions strategy which seemed designed not so much to bring life and freedom and gladness to the unevangelized masses as to provide another opportunity for the unblessed to suffer in an exquisite way.

Today this system of satisfactions and penances is giving way. Even the purest of the evangelicals can no longer hold the line against the milder forms of worldliness.

The devotional disciplines also seem to be coming apart at the seams. But we need not fear that we who are unblessed will lack opportunity for strenuous exercise. The personal legalism of the past is becoming the social legalism of the present, and the old maledictions—"no, no" and "woe, woe"—are giving way not to a free acceptance of social responsibility but to an up-tight and nagging prophetism in the style of John the Baptist.

If I understand Jesus, he did not intend this gymnastic faith. He promised not an impossible yoke and an intolerable burden but an easy yoke and a light burden. What did he really intend? Well, he certainly did not rule out suffering and death. He invited us to take up our cross daily and to follow him. But the cross seems not to have been a burden we were to impose on ourselves out of guilt, but the consequence of our encounter with the world while his companions. Because of his presence, such an encounter—no matter how serious, bitter, and painful—would not be too much for us. In contrast to a life without him, it would be easy and light.

What then has gone wrong? Why did Christianity within a few decades of its origin depart from the gospel of our Lord and the insights of Paul and develop a new legalism, which, although purged from many of the ceremonial rules of the Jewish religion, was nevertheless censorious, gymnastic, resentful, and seriously hung-up in its view of sexuality and the created order? Why did the followers of Jesus shift the emphasis away from the party to the slave camp, from blessedness, from grace to law? Why the new thing, or the old warmed-over thing, the raised magisterial index finger we notice in *The Shepherd of Hermas,* the feverish writings of Tertullian, and even the kindlier admonitions of Clement of Alexandria? Within two hundred years of Pentecost the Holy Spirit has become a caged bird, and the joyous celebration an un-party.

I do not want to pose as a philosopher of history who has

discovered the final answer to this vexing question. But it is possible to discern a trend as the church moves into the second century.

The gospel began as God's means for dealing with guilt. The kerygma, or proclamation, which is the substance of apostolic preaching, announced God's mighty acts in Jesus Christ culminating in the resurrection and exaltation of our Lord. The human response to these acts is outlined in Acts 2:

> When the people heard this [that is, the kerygma], they were deeply troubled, and said to Peter and the other apostles, "What shall we do brothers?" Peter said to them: "Turn away from your sins, each one of you, and be baptized in the name of Jesus Christ, so that your sins will be forgiven; and you will receive God's gift, the Holy Spirit" (Acts 2:37-38, TEV).

The essential good news is God's graciousness as revealed in Jesus. When we hear it proclaimed, we realize that it is a gift which we very much need in order to deal with our sins and failures. The gospel invites us to die and to rise to newness of life in Christ. Theology talks about justification—being made righteous by God's act. Because of Jesus we are now O.K. We have a new identity in Jesus—a new name—which makes our identity as persons O.K. and makes us O.K. persons.[2]

But we remain human beings; we are not supermen. We do not sin for the purpose of receiving grace but we sin—again and again. Hence we must constantly proclaim or have proclaimed for us both our humanity and our O.K.ness in Jesus. The Holy Spirit performs this work among us through the fellowship. It is, however, possible to err in two directions: (1) If we forget that we are human and that we carry our treasure in common clay pots, we fall into the trap of self-righteousness. (2) If we assume that our humanity can stay human by being left to itself, we develop a secular arrogance.

We spoke of discerning a trend. Rather early the church in its fear of making liberty an occasion for license, that is, of antinomianism (against-lawness), opted for a holiness which, in effect, sought to live above humanity. In the later Epistles of the New Testament, notably Titus, 1 & 2 Timothy, Jude and 2 Peter, the paradox of the treasure in earthen vessels has been set aside in favor of a Christianity which knows what to believe and how to act. It still remembers a savior who provided forgiveness from past sins, but it now expects pure doctrine and faultless behavior of those who are to inherit the salvation to come.

The world is now divided simply into two camps: the orthodox Christian with his goodness, holiness, self-control, and sexual purity; his modest, sensible and sober wife; and his well-managed and obedient children on the one side; on the other the unbeliever and profligate who holds "destructive, untrue doctrines" and who lives according to his passions and bodily lusts. Singled out for reprobation in particular are the false teachers "who are like dried-up springs, like clouds blown along by a storm." Because they lead people astray, no punishment is too severe for them. "They will be destroyed like wild animals" (2 Peter 2:12, 17, TEV); they will suffer destruction in fire like Sodom and Gomorrah.

It is well to be charitable and to understand the trials of the church in the closing decades of the first and the opening decades of the second century. In periods of such intense pressures both from confused doctrines and an arrogant libertinism, the paradoxes tend to get flattened out and the Christian message with its fragile counterpoint gets reduced to a pious moralism.

But though the shift in emphasis is understandable and forgivable, the result is no less disastrous. What emerges in the second century is the outline of the un-party, a church which is beginning to forget grace as a life style and which is learning to induce and manipulate guilt to retain the integrity of the institution.

I once thought that the institution was the villain and order the enemy of freedom, but it is clear that each needs the other. Life would be impossible without rationality and habit. And because these are so integral to our ordinary lives, we must expect the conceptualization and ritualization also of religious happening. In a profound passage on the meaning of the oral tradition in poetry, C. S. Lewis says of ritual:

> Ritual is a pattern imposed on the mere flux of our feelings by reason and will which renders pleasures less fugitive and griefs more endurable, which hands over to the power of wise custom the task (to which the individuals and his moods are so inadequate) of being festive or sober, gay or reverent, when we choose to be, and not at the bidding of chance.[3]

It was thus inevitable and good that the life Jesus brought should be expressed, continued, and disseminated through various forms. Faith statements, even in their absurdity, contradiction, and paradox, needed to be made consistent, as far as possible; worship required a certain kind of standardization of usage; teaching about the Jesus walk must be purged of both moralism and libertinism; the overseeing of doctrine, rite, and behavior needed responsible responsibility in the appointment and continuation of leadership.

There was nothing intrinsically wrong in the development of order if the order had been used to continue the Jesus message. The Jesus message even in its Pauline and Johannine interpretations did not divide the world into the goodies and the baddies. It invited all men to share in the gift of O.K.ness (grace), but it was aware of the infinite complexity of man's nature and of its beautiful uncontrollability. It was aware that human freedom made failure and sin inevitable and that O.K.ness (grace) did not make men permanently good or permanently anything.

What went wrong was not so much that the church institutionalized itself as that it fell into the error of the goodies and baddies. By pointing a monitory finger at the baddies (the lapsed in the persecutions) and raising the goodies (the martyrs) to a superhuman rank, it was able to induce guilt and increasingly to manipulate it.

It now became important to "make it" with the institutional church, to be the dutiful elder brother, to be good, humble and obedient, and when lapses occurred to provide the necessary compensations. To be a churchman was no longer to be a recipient of O.K.ness in the company of Jesus, but to pay one's debts. There were several of them:

(1) To be orthodox, to believe the right thing. It is, I think, wrong to assume that in the institutional church people confessed the "right things" only or primarily out of the need to conform or out of fear. A more probable motive for unyielding orthodoxy was guilt. To desert the "faith" was to dishonor father and mother. To believe unquestioningly and to reject doubt was to be a dutiful child. (In this connection the contrast between the early and late Epistles of the New Testament is instructive. In the earlier ones, that is, Colossians and Ephesians, children are exhorted to be obedient to their parents, but there are balancing responsibilities for parents. In 1 Timothy 3:2–5 (TEV) the tone has changed: "A church leader . . . must be able to manage his own family well, and make his children obey him with all respect. For if a man does not know how to manage his own family, how can he take care of the Church of God?" A "managing" kind of parent was

sure to make orthodoxy a test not only of loyalty to God but of fidelity to the family. And this hold on the child's guilt was a source of powerful control.

(2) To worship regularly. The burdensome ceremonial obligations of the Jewish faith were soon mirrored in the activity of Christians. Regular attendance at worship and a range of private religious exercises were ways of proving one's faithfulness. Prayer became a means of satisfying the divine demand.

(3) To behave properly. There were several ways in which the debt could be paid. There was the ordinary observance of the divine command; personal decency; meeting obligations to family, friends, and community. But there was also extraordinary behavior: being a *confessor* during the persecutions and later becoming a *member* of a religious community or fighting in a holy war. Protestants have not been too sympathetic toward this meritorious righteousness and have no doubt exaggerated its legalistic tendencies, but the fact remains that much Christian behavior in the Middle Ages was motivated by guilt which the church both induced and manipulated.

(4) To be obedient to the institution. Beyond the demands for sound doctrine, observance of public worship, and proper conduct, the church exacted obedience. The familial language of the religious organization—pope (papa), father, brother, sister, child—suggests that the church sought to duplicate within its structure the dynamics of the natural family with a strong emphasis on duty and obedience.

Martin Luther and the other reformers reacted against this theology of guilt and debt, and reaffirmed the theology of O.K.ness and the freedom of the Christian man. The Reformation was thus a tremendous breakthrough for New Testament faith. Dogma was replaced by trust; worship was simplified to mean only the faithful proclamation of the Word and the right administration of the sacraments; private prayer was no longer an obligation or a means of temporal satisfaction but only personal communion with God; the authority for behavior was shifted from councils and canons to the Scriptures; and the authorities and mediative machinery of the church which had been the province largely of the priesthood were given to all believers.

But despite its magnitude, the triumph was short-lived. Orthodoxy came back with a new twist in the sixteenth and seventeenth centuries; Puritanism and Pietism, emerging in the seventeenth century, provided a theology of guilt and debt. There were, of course, moments of freedom. Both the Puritans and the Pietists shifted the emphasis from doctrine to experience, and a careful reading of the books and pamphlets which emerged in the religiously turbulent years of the seventeenth century suggests a somber joy in the midst of the scrutiny of conscience.

Count Nikolaus von Zinzendorf, the father of the modern Moravian Church, in reaction from the dourness of the Pietists insisted that to be a Christian was not to be pious but to be joyous. He so emphasized the party that the Moravians for a time fell into unhappy excesses.

English Methodism and evangelicalism, both highly significant for the development of Anglo-American revivalism of the nineteenth century, struggled with the meaning of joy but seem to have left the impression of gloom in the minds of some of their contemporaries. Fielding's jibe at Methodism is familiar.*

* "Being arrived here, they chose for their house of entertainment the sign of the Bell, an excellent house indeed, and which I do most seriously recommend to every reader who shall visit this ancient city.

The practical effect, if not the theological intention, of the movements which branched out from Puritanism and Pietism has been to perpetuate the un-party. The control, the strenuousness, the sobriety, the devotional intensity, the binding regimen of services and meetings have created a profound conviction both inside and outside the church that the evangelical church is not a party at all, but a drill hall where hilarity is occasional and accidental and where the purpose is to fashion well-disciplined soldiers for the holy war.

It is an irony of history that Protestantism, which reintroduced the party with its emphasis on freedom and joy in contrast to the up-tightness and strenuousness of fifteenth-century Roman Catholicism, so soon yielded to the attraction of the un-party and became, in effect, a rebirth of Roman religiousness without the latter's aesthetic or intellectual power. There is an almost undeviating line from first-century Jewish

---

The master of it is brother to the great preacher Whitefield; but is absolutely untainted with the pernicious principles of Methodism, or of any other heretical sect. He is indeed a very honest plain man, and, in my opinion, not likely to create any disturbance either in church or state. His wife hath, I believe, had much pretension to beauty, and is still a very fine woman. Her person and deportment might have made a shining figure in the politest assemblies; but though she must be conscious of this and many other perfections, she seems perfectly contented with, and resigned to, that state of life to which she is called; and this resignation is entirely owing to the prudence and wisdom of her temper; for she is at present as free from any Methodistical notions as her husband; I say at present; for she freely confesses that her brother's documents made at first some impression upon her, and that she had put herself to the expense of a long hood, in order to attend the extraordinary emotions of the Spirit; but having found, during an experience of three weeks, no emotions, she says, worth a farthing, she very wisely laid by her hood and abandoned the sect. To be concise, she is a very friendly, good-natured woman; and so industrious to oblige, that the guests must be of a very morose disposition who are not extremely well satisfied in her house." Henry Fielding, *The History of Tom Jones* (New York: Modern Library), p. 361.

Pharisaism through Jude and 2 Peter, medieval monasticism, Puritanism, and Pietism down to present-day evangelicals and up tight activists, which suggests that law and grace are an unchanging antinomy and that the way to the party is not provided by conceptual theology no matter how grace-oriented, but by a revelation through people, in whatever context, who are being transformed by the O.K.ness of Jesus into new beings.

Chapter 12

The
Un-party

*(a short digression
into personal history)*

Another melancholy effect of the institutionalizing of the church (the un-party) is the erosion of humanity. The churchman feels the need to make himself more than human. He becomes religious or pious; worse still he demands religiousness and piety of his children. Instead of New Testament saintliness, which is the paradoxical indwelling of humanity by the Holy Spirit, he develops *sanctity,* which in the Roman, Orthodox, and Protestant traditions means not merely living above sin but above humanness.

The concomitants of sanctity are humility and, appropriately, other-worldliness.

I grew up under the influence of this model. I was taught to be humble. Fear of pride and worldliness dominated my life, and I grew up distrustful of the good things in the life around me as well as of my own gifts. I shared in the unblessedness of the nonconformist culture.

In my particular tradition there was a strong emphasis on the last things and on the unexpected and catastrophic return of Christ. At any moment "this goodly frame, the earth," might be given to the flames, and the living and dead summoned for the last judgment. I understand that for the adults, ground as they were under the wheel of poverty, illness, and the shame of their class, such a consummation was devoutly to be wished. I do not blame them for their longings to be with Christ and to be rid once and for all of their small circumstances, the gray monotony and laboriousness of their days, the burden of a flesh with which they never came to terms, the fear of illness and of death. If they thought of a party at all, it was on the other side of death.

But for me as a child the earth was, in spite of poverty, hunger, and a heavy dose of illness, a place I was loath to lose. We lived during my early childhood in a scenic part of Sweden, and my waking hours were filled with the impact of a thousand images: spruce forests with carpets of moss and mystical tarns; moors with purple heather; birches stretching their white branches and vivid green toward a sky which burned blue; and small meadows medallioned with flowers and framed by stone walls which made them wonderfully secure and tucked away—like a corner of paradise.

There were the ingenious contrivances of man: a railroad which bisected the village and on which neatly tailored steam locomotives drew their strings of cars to Stockholm and Malmö; a sawmill which provided stacks of freshly cut boards and mountains of fragrant sawdust; a nail factory filled with mysterious whirrs and chuffs, spinning wheels and slapping belts; and marvel of marvels for a child, a miniature railroad with a doll-sized engine and toy tracks, which brought peat bales in from the bogs and deposited them at a railroad siding.

And there was the farm, a mile away and through the woods, a perfect miracle of old buildings with creaking doors, hay mows where the summer sunlight knifed through cracks between the century-old boards; a stable hung with ancient harnesses and a treasury of sleigh bells; a byre shared by the cows, living and breathing and ruminating in their own secret rhythm, and by the sheep and lambs who spoke to me not symbolically but directly of the heavenly sheepfold.

But the heart of the farm for me was the horses. Time would fail me if I told of all the ways they spoke to me. I loved their stateliness, the way they threw their heads and tossed their manes; I loved their stamping, the wild peril of their hooves, their bared teeth, the fleck of foam at the corners of their mouths; I loved their glossy coats, the ripple of muscles, their thrust against the harness, the curving of their necks under the rein; and I loved their smell, spare and clean. Unlike the pigs who relished a miscellaneous diet of slops with an offensive slurpiness and stink, the horses limited themselves to hay and grain—dry, clean, rustling things with the fragrance of summer in them.

But my image of the world was not limited to the cute, the blue, and the tidy. Under the flashes of beauty which transported my child soul, there was a bazaar of ordinary impressions which dizzied me with their muchness. I do not discount the pigs entirely. In a way I loved their flopping around in mash and mire as well as their comical squint. I have learned from specialists that pigs are neither relaxed nor dirty. They are supposed to be neurotic and to thrive on clean styes. I probably misunderstood them, but these pink, fat creatures so pillowy and billowy were a happy denial of some of the uptightness I sensed in many adults.

Because I lived in the country and had never read William

Wordsworth on the moral influence of a vernal wood, I accepted rather early that much of rural life is unpretty and gross. There were dung heaps with pools of nauseating liquid; there was a place behind my uncle's slaughterhouse with a smell of old blood and entrails and the melancholy grins of beast skulls; there was a whole range of unmanageable feelings running from shyness to outrage which stirred in my body and mind; there was sexuality, dealt with pedagogically by my mother but among the citizens pitched back and forth with innuendo and choking laughter; a bloody, panting, whimpering thing called birth went on in the stables and byres, so did an unbloody, groaning thing called death; I was troubled by the assumed connection between words and fragments of verse which I learned from my older friends and did not fully understand and the big-bellied women I encountered on the roads of the village.

There was furthermore the bewildering, fascinating, and ultimately depressing world of the machine. The motorcycles, touring cars, and flying machines which passed through or over our village now and then were touched with divinity, but other machines seemed to me cold, dirty, noisy, unapproachable, and above all else boring. My father was an industrial engineer and I remember trying to extract some pulp and juice from the technical catalogues and journals which came our way, but after a few pages I was overwhelmed by their dullness. I will except from the charge of dullness the trains which chuffed through our villages on the main line, will except them for their glowing fires and their coaches strung out like jewels. Their elegant interiors, filled with what must have been dukes and princes, provided glimpses of a world beyond the green horizon. But the coal, soot, grease, cinders, and rust; the pale, smudged faces and soiled clothing; the thunder and crash of the big machines in the factory world—all these things alienated me.

Yet in their everydayness I loved them also.

This was my child world and I loved it. Even when it bored me, I honored it and did not want to lose it. Hence, I resented that exaggerated unblessed other-worldliness which I encountered not so much in my home as in the chapel where we worshiped. There, despite some truly inspiring moments, the hymns were often about the miseries of earth and the contrasting joys of heaven.

I am convinced that at heart all of us welcome transcendence. I agree with C. S. Lewis that perhaps heaven is all any one of us really wants. But if this is true, it has got to be a discovery each one makes for himself. An adult may so interrelate the brittleness and beauty of earth and the rapture of the coming age that the one does not neutralize the other. But a child can't. He makes the whole business into either/or. And I resented what I felt was an insult piled on the good earth by Christians.

Most of the time we got the message of the fragile world which could like an eggshell cave in any moment. On Ephiphany Day when I was eight years old, the heavens suddenly were lighted with the fretted fires of the northern lights, a very unusual phenomenon in our part of the country. We were standing in the garden with my mother, and with her enthusiasm for the glories of creation she was talking about the majesty of God. Suddenly the air was rent with the loud voice of a man who came running up the path screaming, "The heavens are burning! Jesus is coming!" He was an itinerant evangelist holding services in the local chapel. His outburst frightened us children out of our wits. The fiery heavens were suddenly a threat rather than a promise, and we scurried into the house and the safety of our beds.

It must have been against this background that a few weeks later I had my first real encounter with the Creator. As I now remember it, I lived in despair. I really loved the earth and its glories, but I was afraid to tilt my frail lance against all the concentrated conviction about the impermanence of things. My mother and I empathized about the beauty of the world, but I was afraid that she also would consider my feelings childish and perhaps irreverent. So I kept them to myself.

Then one January morning I walked alone through the woods to the farm. It was a perfect winter day. The sun was just rising above a fringe of spruces, and the snow on the branches sparkled happily. There was fresh snow on the road, and I was the first to walk on it. To my right the blue railroad tracks swung south in a graceful arc. And above me the sky was coldly blue and free of clouds. It was very quiet.

I was so overwhelmed by the beauty of the world and so grateful to God for having made it that way that I got down on my knees in the snow and thanked him. Years later when I read Edna St. Vincent Millay's lines

> Lord, I do fear
> Thou'st made the world too beautiful this year.
> My soul is all but out of me . . .[1]

they served as a touchstone for my childish feeling.

The years have a way of deceiving us, but I feel that in those moments in the forest I was asking God to be on my side in my struggle against those who thought ill of the world. I wanted him to give me the assurance that his creation was worth investing in and that I was really at the party.

To be a humble Christian in my childhood meant also being diffident about your gifts. Very diffident. It was characteristic of the community in which I grew up to be shy about the achievements of one's kin To that shyness my father added the dimension of Christian lowliness. My mother, who was blessed by her family, also had an upcountry freedom about the family laurels, but my father suffered real pain if anyone lauded his children, especially in their presence. Praise was supposed to lead to overweening pride. Even after we were adults it was consequently impossible for either my brother or me to get any sort of positive evaluation of our writing (and both of us wrote copiously) or of any other achievement from him.

Rather early I began to witness publicly. I was fairly articulate and managed as a fifteen-sixteen-year-old to make sense on my feet in congregational meetings. This led some people in the church to suggest that I should consider the ministry. But all this filled my father with intense embarrassment. He never alluded to my speaking, and I felt that the whole subject was shameful to him as if I had had an infirmity. I consequently backed off. I had learned to be humble and I believe that my father thought that any encouragement he could give me would only bring me to the end of Ozymandias or Herod the Great. As a result of this I still have a terrible time accepting affirmation or appreciation. I don't like to be thanked publicly; at least I feel guilty about it. To be insensitive to praise, to protest expressions of gratitude—this I learned, is the way the Christian dies. It used to be summed up admirably in a gospel song heard frequently in my youth.

> I would be nothing, nothing, nothing,
> Thou shalt be all in all.

Christian humility also extended to money. Money was not supposed to get mixed up with our life, especially our witness. I consequently entered the ministry with a neurotic feeling about money. Unconsciously I wanted it, but at the conscious level I refused it as being unworthy of a servant of Christ. Now the beautiful thing about Jesus was that he had no hang-ups about either humility or money. When he talks about humility, he means something entirely different from what I meant. When he talks about money it is not as if he hated the stuff. He knows, of course, that some people let money foul them up and that some put money before people. But Jesus has a nice, healthy, unguilty feeling about money, its value and use. Nowhere do I see him turn money down as if it were dirty in and of itself.

But in my earlier years I thought it was dirty. At that time it was fairly common for the various special services of the minister to be compensated for by a fee or honorarium. Baptisms, weddings, and funerals were good for five or ten dollars depending on the affluence of the person being served. It was probably not a good system, but considering the salary level of the clergyman, it was certainly not anything to make a big deal about. But I had to make it a big deal. My neurotic refusal to accept anything for these functions may have made some sense if I had applied it to widows and orphans. But I applied it to all. I would not let the happy bridegroom, for whom the fee may have served as giving hostages to fortune, pay me. I would not let the wealthy apostate son who was burying his mother and may have needed some help in atoning for his guilt, cross my palm. I was simply above money. And poor as I was, I saw the refusal as a form of dying.

Chapter 13

Come
to
the
Party

It should now be apparent that if I once believed that the Protestant doctrine of humility and humiliation was an adequate interpretation of Christian death and resurrection, I no longer believe it. I don't believe that the ego should be killed or die, and even if I did believe in the necessity of that kind of death, I see the futility of bringing it about. The biggest ego trip in the world is the guilty effort to deny the ego. Even Paul's words to the Galatians which once meant ego-death no longer mean that to me. "I have been crucified with Christ; the life I now live is not my life, but the life which Christ lives in me; and my present bodily life is lived by faith in the Son of God, who loved me and sacrificed himself for me" (Gal. 2:20, NEB).

What then do death and resurrection mean? Or at least, what do they mean to me?

I think death means not the destruction of the ego but the

unguilty acceptance of its existence. I think death means climbing down from the perch of holiness, piety, self-denial, or
whatever form the delusion that we can be superhuman takes,
and simply accepting our humanity. I believe that Saul's conversion on the way to Damascus was the acceptance of the
fact that his pharisaic zeal was actually an attack on God, that
instead of supporting God's work of salvation in the world
Saul was, in fact, obstructing it. And he was obstructing it by
living in his competence as a religious leader and not in his
humanity. The Saul who is discovered by Ananias in the house
of Judas in Straight Street is not a prayer warrior who is
charting a course of international evangelism but a blind and
frightened man who has to begin where all of us must begin—
in the recognition that he is Saul, no more and no less.

This recognition of my humanity—my willingness to accept in myself the whole range of frailties flesh is heir to and
to present myself vulnerably to the world—is my death and my
dying. It is not to be humble or modest or unassuming; it is
not to lie about my gifts or to lie about anything. It is to be
real, to be myself. If I am the Apostle Paul, it is to be Paul:
bristly, sensitive, neurotic, angry, warm, loving, grateful, creative, joyous, rhapsodic. If I am Augustine, it is to be Augustine;
volcanic, profound, at once celestial and terrestrial, at once
erotic and ecstatic, at once the burning intellect and the luminous heart. Death means being where I am. It means not
donning masks or climbing on stilts, but being incorrigibly
what I am.

Death means a willingness to accept the other person in the
full dimension of his humanity. It means the end of an idealism
which endows me with a helper role and makes me the in-
variable gift-giver, the minister, the servant. My gift to the
other has meaning only if we are fellow human beings and

if his gift honestly enriches me. It's only when I understand and accept at gut level that I need other people as much as they need me that I can begin to relate to them.

Death means the acceptance of the team, the fellowship (koinonia) as an indispensable part of my life. It means that I need the team to affirm and support me, to pray with me and for me, to weep with me when I weep and to rejoice with me when I rejoice. But I also need it to keep me human. I need a love so strong that within its circle I can be told and accept the worst and the best about myself.

The team is not the people I like, or work with, or even worship with. The team is a band of people under the guidance of the Holy Spirit who have chosen me and whom I have chosen, because in their company I can be most myself.

The composition of this team does not remain changeless. It is constantly being eroded by time and change and is yet constantly renewed. In the measure that the team becomes meaningful to me as the new family of blessing I am able to be more and more inclusive in my loves. Because the team lets me be human, I can be human toward more and more people. Thus, in a real sense, the church becomes catholic (universal).

But the team continues to exist only in a dimension of such radical honesty that it is invariably tempted to compromise itself and become something less than a team. Because death is so painful, the team may ritualize it. Because piety is an easier stance than humanity, the team may go pious. Because love is, as Dante said, a "lord of terrible aspect," the team may decide to settle for courtesy or even comity. When that happens, creative dying dies and so does new life.

To die is also to level, to tell it like it is. This means the end of the sermon as a ritualized performance at the un-party and the beginning of communication by sharing and modeling. I have tried elsewhere to set this kind of communication into the new life style which is everywhere emerging:

> Perhaps the truth is that this style of life is not taught but caught. You do not communicate it by getting up and delivering a monologue about it. You do not convey it by writing an article about it. The standard educational process (although this too is changing) is pouring a full notebook into an empty one. One man speaks and several listen. The larger the audience and the more important the speaker, the more anonymous and uninvolved the listener.
>
> We have come to think that you present the Christian life style most effectively by modeling and sharing. You let people witness death and resurrection.
>
> Traditional communication proceeds from planning a talk to drafting a manuscript of it to polishing it to rehearsing it to presenting it. It is an act from which much of the anxiety has been purged. If it goes well, you repeat it, over and over again.
>
> But to model is to share the present hurt and the present joy. It is to speak out of a raw throat and quivering nerves or out of a current jubilation with laughter shaking the spirit. It is to break the loaf of life and to pass around pieces. And it is to do this in such a way that people respond by a free act of sharing.
>
> Because we are Christians we believe that the model of this kind of communication is the Biblical word. Jesus did not come to hand us a theology but to reveal God in what he was and what he did. Everywhere he affirmed his humanity in how he dealt with people and circumstances, and everywhere the humanity was the dying—the grain of wheat which fell in the ground and died and did not abide alone.[1]

The Bible can be used doctrinally or relationally—it can be subject matter which I master and which I dish out with my particular kind of theological-literary-anecdotal-cultural sauce and seasoning; or it can be a life style—death and resurrection. We have been surfeited with a doctrinal biblicism which is objective and relatively safe. But we have not had very much of the relational Bible which demands a radical identification with the biblical character and the biblical situation. The kind of dying we are talking about implies such identification. I see myself in Peter and Saul and Mary Magdalene and Ananias and Sapphira and Judas, and even such sad, brittle people as Caiaphas, Pontius Pilate, and Herod. I also identify myself with the fun people in the Scriptures—those who have something going for them—the dancing David, Miriam, Job dreaming about crocodiles and wild asses and the treasures of the snow, and some anonymous psalmists who heard the earth singing. Although when you get right down to it, it's hard to keep the sad and the glad separate.

Death also means accepting the risk of being human. Risking is not crossing Niagara Falls on a tight rope (unless you need to) or going on a mission to the cannibals. It is not "the royal road to adventure." Risking is living life and building relationships without knowing the end from the beginning. It is giving a gift or stepping toward someone without sure knowledge how the act will be received.

In the Western world we have developed the perfect gift culture. That is, we have washed the risk out of giving. We have unbelievably intricate arrangements to guarantee that a gift is not superfluous or unwanted. Because we do not want to suffer the smart of rejection or ridicule, we cautiously tailor what we do to what we know about the receiver. And we create a sterile atmosphere around those festivities which ought to be wild and whirling with joy and love.

We have also developed a perfect worship culture in which the risk has been eliminated from our adoration of God. Presently, thank God, our sanctuaries are being invaded by guitars, split infinitives, poor rhymes, and everyday clothes.

But for many years even the evangelical churches have labored to remove the unpredictable from public services. I have had my share in the perfection of homiletic technique, the elaboration of artistically safe liturgies, the construction of frozen beauty in sanctuaries. In reaction to a woolly evangelical past full of praise Gods, hallelujahs, badly tuned guitars, altar calls, and corny gospel songs, I joined the formalists, only to discover that I had scrubbed the happening. What I got was efficiency in worship without effectiveness. For years under the ministration of myself and those whom I trained, people got stiff necks and tired brains. Very few were turned on toward God, and precious few got a taste of the joy and juice of being alive.

Death is also celebration. It means to accept everything as a gift. It's like going to a party and knowing that someone else has paid for the candles, the food, the wine; it's knowing that nothing I can ever do will bring this about, but that it's O.K., and all I need to do is to accept: to eat, to drink, to sing, to play, to love, to be.

You may ask where Jesus comes into all this. All I can say is that the whole thing is a Jesus thing. It's all possible because he has taken away the curse and blessed us. He has brought us back into the new family, the family of blessing. Because of Jesus we are home free.

Because God became human in Jesus, I can dare to be no more than myself and to accept everything from his hand.

Because of Jesus' love and acceptance of me, I can begin in a fumbling way to accept others and to love even those who have a tough time loving me.

Because of Jesus, the team is possible. The love, the interdependence, the honesty, the suffering together, the risking are his gifts to us. That is why the team is called the body of Jesus.

Because of Jesus' risking to be human and the price he paid for me, I can risk being human and have freedom to fail.

Because Jesus hosted a party in which he himself was bread and wine and in which he gave even the deniers and betrayers to eat and drink, I have the courage to come to the party and to be with him and all his blessed and unblessed forever.

Appendix
and
Notes

Appendix

The question of the "group" or "team" needs more attention than I can give it in these pages. Bigness is a problem in the institutional church, but it would be unfortunate if the emphasis on "small grouping" were thought to refer merely to size. The key to the group or team process is not size but personal interaction. A small congregation or Bible class can be just as deadly as a large one if the flow of communication is in only one direction.

What needs to be emphasized is the dynamics. I have sometimes felt that a new church history should be written from the viewpoint of the group process. There are models of group activity scattered throughout the history of the Christian movement which suggest that we are not so much creating the new as rediscovering the old.

Apparently the synagogue service in Jesus' day allowed for participation and interaction. S. MacLean Gilmour, commenting on Jesus' synagogue visit in Luke 4, writes,

Worship in a Palestinian synagogue consisted of the recitation of the Shema, a prayer, a fixed lection from the Law, a free lection from the Prophets, an explanation and application of one or both of the scriptural passages, and a blessing by a priest or prayer by a layman. The scripture was read in Hebrew, but a translator turned it, verse by verse, into Aramaic. There was no official "minister." An invitation to read and to preach could be extended by the ruling elders to any competent members of the congregation or visitor (cf. Acts 13:15). It was the practice to stand up to read, and to sit down to preach (vv. 20–21).[1]

What we have preserved from the group life of Jesus and his disciples suggests that although Jesus occupied the role of teacher in a peripatetic school of disciples, there was considerable participation on the part of the Twelve at least in the posing of questions.

After Pentecost the disciples seem to have followed a variety of practices within the group itself, although much speaks for the continuation of some of the synagogual practices with which they were familiar. Acts tells us that they proclaimed the gospel, baptized, and performed miracles among those outside the fellowship. Among themselves they seem to have recalled the acts and words of Jesus, related these to the writings of Scripture available to them, prayed, sung, and shared in some type of eucharistic meal. There must also have been considerable interaction about the "commune" itself. We know that there was controversey between Greek-speaking and native Jews about the distribution of funds (Acts 6:1).

In 1 Corinthians Paul gives us a glimpse of group life and worship as it must have existed in a Christian congregation in the middle of the first century. Already there is a procedure to which Paul can refer. Perhaps, since there was strong influence from the synagogue (Acts 18:5–8) in Corinth, the worship followed some of the traditional Jewish patterns. But there were some significant additions in the form of glossolalia and prophecy with which the Apostle deals. Paul writes:

> What then, brethren? When you come together, each one has a hymn, a lesson, a revelation, a tongue, or an interpretation. Let all things be done for edification. If any speak in a tongue, let

there be only two or at most three, and each in turn; and let one interpret. But if there is no one to interpret, let each of them keep silence in church and speak to himself and to God. Let two or three prophets speak, and let the others weigh what is said. If a revelation is made to another sitting by, let the first be silent. For you can all prophesy one by one, so that all may learn and all be encouraged; and the spirits of prophets are subject to prophets (1 Cor. 14:26–32, RSV).

Somewhere in the group process of the primitive church we must find room for additional activities such as confession, absolution, and excorcism. And there is certainly the beginning of liturgy.

Some scholars see the Apocalypse as a liturgy which could be sung or spoken by a congregation in part or in entirety depending on the circumstances.[2] If the Apocalypse is a message in code, as some scholars believe, the liturgy may have provided a battle cry in the face of Rome and a source of edification for the beleagured fellowship.

The second and third centuries probably saw the formalization of worship along lines established in the first. The synagogue worship with Christian additions became the nucleus of the mass in its traditional two parts, and the growth of the church from handfuls of people to crowds necessitated gathering places and services designed to accommodate many rather than few.

In this complex development it is difficult to determine the precise nature of the group process. How much discussion was there? What was the nature of the sharing? Was it catechetical, with questions and answers, or free? Was the subject matter largely factual and conceptual, or was there spontaneous, affective participation? There are as many answers as there are theological positions. Some scholars feel that the process was

formalized from the first with the apostles providing direction
and with very little input from the group at large; others point
to the numerous controversies alluded to in Acts and the Epistles of the New Testament as well as to references to a more
popular kind of assembly in support of the view that the primitive churches were moderately democratic.*

But whatever the nature of the primitive process, we know
that fairly soon the church became formally and methodologi-
cally a temple with priests doing service at the altar and the
congregation sharing only vicariously in the dialogue between
the celebrant and heaven.

The Reformation introduced a number of new styles of worship and group life, but the emphasis was more upon the
teaching and preaching of the Word by qualified professionals
than on popular participation. Among the English Puritans
and Pilgrims, the emphasis on formal preaching and teaching
continued, but the growth of literacy allowed the development
of dialogue around so-called "cases of conscience." A troubled
questioner addressed a concern to his spiritual guide, and received a voluminous answer. These conversations were then
printed for the edification of other believers.

Toward the end of the seventeenth century Phillip Jacob
Spener, a devout pastor in Frankfurt-am-Main, instituted
groups he called *Collegia Pietatis* (gatherings of piety) for the
purpose of making the Scriptures experientially meaningful to
the laity. There is some evidence that conventicles of this type
had been held previously in Holland and perhaps England.
We don't know the exact format of the *collegia,* but presuma-

* For example, in Acts 15 the participation of the church in both
controversy and decision-making seems fairly evident. And Paul's letters, if we exclude the pastoral Epistles, are filled with references to
group interaction.

bly they were Bible studies conducted by the pastor with opportunity for questions by the laity about the practical meaning of the scriptural word.

In the eighteenth century John Wesley, perhaps with models from the Pietists and Moravians, started his Society. Its rules provided for dividing the society into groups or bands of five or ten persons. The members of the bands spoke "plainly" and "freely" to one another about the "real state" of their hearts. Later the bands were assigned lay leaders and were called classes. The meetings of the classes were devoted to religious conversation and prayer. Wesley, in the interest of separating the "precious from the vile," met the classes every quarter and gave tickets signed by him to those whose "seriousness and good conversation" he approved.

Meanwhile Pietistic and Moravian conventicles spread throughout Europe. They were instrumental in generating and in informing the great revivals in Scandinavia in the eighteenth and nineteenth centuries. To begin with, as in the *collegia* of Spener, the parish pastor was the leader, and the format of the conventicle was not unlike a Bible lecture, but with the laicizing of the church more and more untrained leadership emerged. From the practice of using a lay leader, the burden of whose message was often what God had done for him, developed the more general testimony or "witness" which has characterized evangelicalism both American and European down to the present.

The testimony meeting became stylized rather early. Witnessing turned into a narrative of conversion experiencd long ago or into a recital of a favorite Bible verse. Hence its effectiveness decreased and it was dropped as a congregational practice in all except the most conservative churches.

Frank Buchman, the initiator of the Oxford Group Movement, refashioned the testimony in the direction of greater openness and relevance. The "house parties" which characterized the movement in the 1930s encouraged a degree of openness in witness which shocked the more traditional churches and may have discouraged the group process from developing in them. But it was the value of honest sharing which encouraged the development of the small group movement in its present form.

Notes

Chapter 2
1. "Thou my everlasting portion," Fanny T. Crosby.

Chapter 3
1. Wilbert F. Howard, "The Gospel According to St. John," *The Interpreter's Bible* (Nashville: Abingdon Press, 1952), VIII, 688–89.
2. Quoted in Reinhold Niebuhr, *Interpretation of Christian Ethics* (New York: Harper & Bros., 1935), p. 67.
3. John Milton, *Paradise Lost,* Book II, 257–62.

Chapter 5
1. Dante Alighieri, *Hell,* trans. Dorothy L. Sayers (Baltimore: Penguin Books, 1949), Canto III, ll. 4–6, italics mine.
2. Augustine, *Confessions,* trans. Edward B. Puscy (New York: Pocket Books, 1951), p. 27.
3. Frank Luther Mott and Chester E. Jorgenson, *Benjamin Franklin, Representative Selections* (New York: American Book Co., 1936), p. 78.
4. Henry Fielding, *The History of Tom Jones* (New York: Modern Library), p. 77.
5. Edwin Arlington Robinson, *Nicodemus, A Book of Poems* (New York: The Macmillan Co., 1932), p. 13.

Chapter 6
1. Cecil Frances Alexander, "There Is a Green Hill Far Away."

Chapter 7
1. Etienne Gilson, *The Philosophy of St. Bonaventure,* trans. Dom Illtyd Trethowan (New York: Sheed & Ward, 1940), pp. 55–65.

Chapter 8
1. Augustine, op. cit., pp. 168–70, passim.
2. J. D. Salinger, *The Catcher in the Rye* (New York: Bantam Books, 1969), p. 99.

3. T. S. Eliot, "Morning at the Window," *Collected Poems 1909–1962* (New York: Harcourt, Brace, Jovanovich, 1962), p. 19.

Chapter 9

1. See Arthur Janov, *Primal Scream: A Revolutionary Cure for Neurosis* (New York: G. P. Putnam, Sons, 1970).

Chapter 10

1. "Shepherd Boy's Song," *Pilgrim's Progress,* Part II.
2. See "The Un-Party," pp. 159–60.

Chapter 11

1. Arthur Guiterman, "Hills," *The Mirthful Lyre* (New York: Harper & Bros., 1918).
2. Thomas A. Harris, *I'm OK—You're OK: A Practical Guide to Transactional Analysis* (New York: Harper & Row, 1969), is an excellent psychological statement of a profound theological truth.
3. C. S. Lewis, *Preface to Paradise Lost* (Oxford: Oxford University Press, 1942).

Chapter 12

1. Edna St. Vincent Millay, "God's World," *Renascence* (New York: Harper & Bros., 1917).

Chapter 13

1. Faith at Work Fellowship Letter, *Open Circle,* March 1971, Volume 4, Number 1.

Appendix

1. Exegesis of Luke 4:16–30 in *The Interpreter's Bible* (Nashville: Abingdon Press, 1952), VIII, 89.
2. N. W. Lund, *Chiasmus in the New Testament* (Chapel Hill: University of North Carolina Press, 1942).